sex for money

Lily Moreau

Sex For Money by Lily Moreau

First published by Lily Moreau, 2023

ISBN: 978-1-3999-5273-6

Contents

1

I was on my way to an outcall booking. I've been called out to some dreadful places, but this one was pleasingly upmarket – the St. Pancras Renaissance Hotel. Things were looking up. I could feel my life was starting to get a bit more interesting.

The satnav directed me to the front of the hotel and I drove up the ramp to hotel parking. I looked around at the cars – Bentleys, Maserati and Aston Martins. There was even a bloody Rolls-Royce Silver Ghost, just slung at an angle across two bays. I clocked the tariff on the wall – £15 for three hours – and decided to take my embarrassing fifteen-year-old VW Polo to a quiet road, two blocks behind the hotel. As I walked back, I wished that, one day, I could just roll up to the concierge, throw him my keys and stroll in. That was not happening yet, sadly, so, instead, I was racked with self-consciousness and the new shoes I bought were killing my feet.

The magnificence of the Gothic architecture of the St. Pancras Renaissance was impossible to ignore; my body was trembling and nervous. *What if he doesn't like me? What if I've come all this way and he just sends me home?* My heart was beating fast – I wanted to impress him. I considered how much the hotel room must have cost and how much he was paying me. He must have money. I couldn't blow this opportunity to meet such a rich client and turn him into a regular. To frequent these beautiful places and dress in glamorous clothes was what I wanted, wasn't it? It just seemed so far away from my current reality.

I arrived at the front entrance, cursing my shoes, and, as if the feeling of scrutiny and judgement wasn't enough, I stumbled on the ramp and only just about managed to keep my balance and not fly face-first onto the pavement.

The doorman moved to come help me, but I waved my hands, showing that it was fine. My face was red, and embarrassment was surging though me. I was just glad the client didn't see me make that entrance.

He arrived at the door just seconds later and he had a mobile phone in his hand, ready to give me a call in case he couldn't see me. He smiled, looking at me from the head to toe. 'Hi Lily, I am Mr Handsome.'

I smiled back and gave him a peck on the cheek. 'Nice to meet you.'

'Let's go to the bar and have a few drinks. I'm going to introduce you to my wife.'

I stood there, aghast, trying to see if he was joking. 'What?' I shouted, my legs shaking. 'How? What? Your wife's there? Now?' I was struggling to form a coherent sentence.

'Calm, calm, Lily, behave!' he said, laughing. 'Don't worry, she's not alone either. We are all just here for a bit of fun.'

I gawked, completely unresponsive. I felt the urge to just run away, but I was rooted to the spot. And even if my body was willing, these bloody shoes wouldn't allow a quick getaway.

'Come on, remember the rules: be strong, talk firm, don't show weakness; clients pay, but I am in charge,' I told myself, and regained an element of composure.

The doorman opened the door and ushered us into the lobby. 'Thank you,' I said, smiling. As we walked through the lobby, I couldn't help noticing the sheer grandeur of the place.

We walked through the lobby to the bar, which was carpeted and very luxurious, and approached the glowing gold counter. Mr Handsome led me to a couple who were sitting on stools, sipping vodka and Coke. He introduced me to his wife and her friend.

'Mrs Kinky' was dressed in Chanel and, on first impression, was a very classy, sexy and beautiful lady in her fifties. She gave me a warm hug and, as she grazed my cheek with a kiss, I got a waft of her perfume, which was warm and spicy, but also floral.

Is it Chanel, I wondered, to go with her dress and bag? Either way, like her husband, she had an air about her that only money can bring. Clocking the huge diamond on her left hand, glinting under the lights of the bar, confirmed my assumptions.

And her friend ... well, he was so fit! A good few years younger than Mrs Kinky, he was in a crisp blue shirt, with his sleeves rolled up to reveal a tattooed arm. He smiled, got up from his stool and gave me a big bear hug, squishing my tiny frame into his chest.

The 'Fireman' was a very attentive person, asking questions and taking care to involve everyone in the group. He was friendly and hilarious (especially after a few double gin and tonics) and, whilst I could have easily sat at the bar all night, soaking up the atmosphere, I knew that was not what I was here for, and I started to wonder how the rest of the evening was going to play out.

I was interested to know if Mrs Kinky was bisexual, as then they could be after a foursome. I watched her body language, but I didn't think so; she was focussed on her toy boy – actually, he looked like he might be in his early forties, but still younger than her.

After a few drinks at the bar, we were all suitably relaxed and decided it was time to the evening along. Mr Handsome charged the bill to his suite and we headed to the lift.

Up on the eighth floor, Mr Handsome ushered us into their room. It was enormous – bigger than my entire flat. To me, it was like being inside a palace, with plush carpets, luxurious furniture and an amazing view across London from windows that spanned the full length of the room. Just off the living room, I spotted the bedroom. I poked my head round the door to see a super king-size bed. On the end of it was a small suitcase, open and full of toys – and I'm not talking about jigsaws and board games.

Mr Handsome popped up over my shoulder. 'It's my wife's suitcase,' he said, giggling.

'Hmm, she is a naughty woman,' I replied.

'I have a fetish for seamed stockings,' he told me. 'I requested that you wear them, but you're not.'

'Oh, no, I completely forgot. I am so sorry,' I said, as a wave of panic surged through my stomach. Would he send me straight home?

'Next time,' he replied with a smile, and wandered off.

As we had a drink in the living room, he just came out with it. 'I love anal sex,' he announced to the room. *Here we are*, I think. *My USP* (unique selling point). I needed to impress him now, as I felt I'd made rather too many gaffes so far to keep getting away with it. So, I undressed and Mr Handsome led me into the bedroom. I pushed him down into the chair next to the bed. I assumed the cowgirl position and started to deliver my service.

I could hear moaning and groaning coming from the living room, where Mrs Kinky and the Fireman seemed to be enjoying themselves. After Mr Handsome climaxed, Mrs Kinky and the Fireman walked into the bedroom. He bent her over and started going at her, doggy style, for all he was worth. Mr Handsome was just sitting there, with me on his lap, completely unfazed by what was being acted out in front of him.

'Don't worry, my wife's very naughty. She loves to be fucked hard – and I don't fuck her that hard,' he whispered in my ear.

It had been five hours since I arrived, and it was time to leave. I gathered my stuff, said my goodbyes and, with a big sigh of relief, stepped outside, feeling desperate for fresh air. 'What was going on there?' I wondered, thinking about everything that had happened in the hotel, a husband and wife fucking strangers, watching each other? It didn't seem normal to me.

I walked to my car, thinking that tonight would be as good as it got this week – a five-hour booking. But there would be more to come before the week was out.

Three days later, I got a short email and then an outcall booking request through the website for the next day at ExCel London. It was from a verified member with good feedback. I accepted, as three hours would be great money

The cab left me at the hotel. I walking through the lobby when I got a phone call from Kate, a friend who I'd met at another friend's house, Fernanda, when she was a madam for us a few months prior, before I started working as an independent.

'Fernanda went to Spain,' she said, 'and she's now trying to get back into the UK, but Immigration stopped her. She had her entry denied and she is desperate for someone to get a solicitor or write a letter. Did she call you?'

'No, I haven't spoken to her since I left her house. After all the trouble she has been involved in, what does she expect? No one would be crazy enough to try to help her. I am on my way to visit a client and am already late. I'll call you tomorrow though. Love you,' I said, and hung up the phone.

I had already had too many headaches with Fernanda, and was not interested in helping someone who just messed me around and had no consideration for anyone.

I knocked on the hotel room door and the client opened it. I was facing a well-presented gentleman, possibly in his sixties. I went inside the suite. There was an ice bucket with a bottle of champagne and an envelope on the side with my fee. 'Life is not bad,' I thought.

'Hi Lily, I am Dr Ray, nice to meet you.' He invited me to sit down, pouring champagne in two flutes.

'What brings you to London?' I asked him.

'I am a gynaecologist from Manchester and I'm here for a medical conference,' he replied very politely, with a calm voice.

We were having a quick chat to break the ice, sipping champagne and picking at some strawberries on the table, when he asked me, 'Have you ever squirted before?'

This question made me stop sipping my drink. 'No, never,' I said, looking at him, surprised by the question.

'Men get very intrigued by it,' he said. 'We do not really know exactly why girls do it. I would like to try to make you gush.'

Oh no, what to say? 'Look, I have never squirted in all my life, and I do not believe I can. This service is not on my menu; you are wasting your time and your money. So let's do a deal. I will give you the choice to pay me only for my trip, and I will leave. Don't waste your money. I won't be able to do it.'

'I don't want you to leave. I want to try to get a woman who has never squirted before to do it. I am just asking if you will let me try. Do not worry about my time and my money, or if you do not manage it. I only want to play with my fingers inside you, so I just need to know if you feel comfortable with that,' he said, with a half-serious smile.

I looked at him, surprised that he was asking permission to touch me. The people in Central London were so much better than where I was before.

'Well, I quite like fingers in,' I replied, 'and, honestly, if you could make me squirt, it would be great. My friend Kate does it and it is very sexy.'

He had the advantage of being a gynaecologist and he had gentle hands. He lubricated me before foreplay and then, with his fingers caressing and stimulating inside me, I suddenly felt a strange sensation: he'd hit my G-spot and I didn't know if I wanted to urinate or if I was aroused. It was strange, but far from a bad feeling. His face was very satisfied and he looked at me, smiling. 'Yes, we made it. All women can squirt,' he said.

I left the room and got in a cab parked in front of the hotel. I was hungry, so I asked the driver to stop before we got to my flat and bought some food. I took a walk, admiring the extraordinary architecture of the Natural History Museum. How can anyone not love London? And I was finally there. This beauty was all around me.

I walked, thinking about how intense this week had been. I'd met Mr Handsome and Mrs Kinky and now someone just booked me to use as an experiment and, more importantly, I'd received very generous envelopes – it was so different from the place where I started. I laughed loudly to myself, having no idea that these two bookings would completely change the course of my life.

This was my fairy tale ending. I didn't start out with all this glamour.

2

My first job as a sex worker happened at Fernanda's house, in a very rough area of London, about six months before those bookings. I considered myself lucky in terms of having what was most important to me: the courage to change what I was not happy with and to fight for what I wanted, which was a better financial life.

My body was still under my control. I had been getting to a point in life where I thought I'd pretty much seen and done everything, but no – life continued to give me lessons, challenges and experiences.

Life is full of infinitely peculiar people from all around this world. I'm one of them – a survivor. But I often wonder why we are here. Is it just to exist?

When they hear about escorts, sex workers, prostitutes, people think it's something to be ashamed of.

The word prostitute makes people perplexed in so-called 'regular' society, just as when people used to see a gay couple on the street, for example, and consider them obscene or perverted.

This was in the past; people now are becoming more open-minded. The world is changing amazingly fast and we need to talk about sex work, as the system must change in order to make us free and allow us to have a voice – to show that we are just normal human beings.

Most of the movies we watch about sex workers, escorts or, more commonly, prostitutes present them as victims or addicts, seeing them as obscene and their clients as ugly and nasty villains. Sex as a business is not seen as an appropriate topic of conversation. It is simply wrong and degrading.

London is not like that, though. It is a big box of surprises, a city of opportunities – or the city of your perdition. Life here goes by very fast. It's a cosmopolitan city, the city where the money is, and it is all about choices and making the right decision.

With a bit of luck and determination, you can make it here. It is the place where I want to be, but it also a place where you cannot get stuck. You win, or you lose, because here, everything is difficult and very expensive.

Money. That's what makes people leave their houses every day and go to work. People spend most of their time working, and I chose sex as work.

I choose to do what I do; it turns me on. It makes me feel different from my private personality, as an everyday single mother, who has always submitted to men and struggled to support her daughter financially. When I'm performing sex work, I feel strong and in control. It's exciting to feel like a 'bitch' and far from a poor little thing. Having many punters makes me feel free, as I love sex, and a vanilla guy or a prince on a white horse to blow my mind and save my life is not my desire.

Who doesn't like to make good money?

I felt like I was just one more person in survival mode, who just works and struggles to end of the month. I wanted more than to live in a hypocritical and conformist society where they built a God to dictate what is right or wrong.

What is right and what is wrong, really? We don't get a chance to create our own principles.

One morning, I caught a train to a job centre and walked around after, feeling dizzy from the crowds as I watched all the people running back and forth, going to work, doing whatever, just to get money. Most were like me, just fighting to survive.

We are all just robots who settle for a function, transformed into slaves to the system and to money – and the more we have, the more we need.

And what's the money really for?

Survival, ostentation, social status and pleasure. Most people in this world only have enough money to survive; others live OK, and only a minority really have the luxury to afford ostentation and pleasure.

I wonder constantly, how do we allow ourselves to accept a system built on the mindset that it is normal to pay for food and water, which are primary necessities? Still, we must pay for it all. But the system makes us believe that it is wrong when someone pays for sex as a pleasure.

Often – not just once or twice – guys get so repentant after they explode in sex, as they feel so guilty and full of regret. But it is easy to say 'Oh, it's so wrong' after having enjoyed a deep orgasm.

Why does society condemn selling sex, when everything else is for sale?

I was born in Brazil, of Japanese and Spanish descent. I left Brazil twenty-five years ago, when I was a teenager, and moved to Japan with my dad. I did not go to university, as I had no way to pay for a private education, and found out early how good it was to have money to pay for my own things. I found out I liked travelling and being able to pay my own bills. Financially, I could afford to do a few things back then. But when I was no longer young, a raising a child on my own, it was not enough. I found that I needed money quickly if I didn't want to die poor. Sadly, I didn't think about this when I was younger.

I lived in many countries after I left Japan. Before arriving in the UK, fourteen years ago now, I decided to end my marriage, after nine years together.

My ex-husband was sixteen years older than me and a very handsome, charming gentleman. I was a young single mother. In our first five years together, he made me the happiest woman in the world and was a great father to my daughter.

I felt I had finally found the right one and I was so happy. He had a lot of experience and he shared it with me. I was learning so much, but then, after five years together, as many couples do, we entered the boring stage, and he entered major depression. The treatment made him a miserable person, always in a bad mood and so negative. Because of the drug therapy, he completely lost his sexual appetite. I saw myself as too young to deal with all of his problems.

Depression is a powerful monster, who digs a deep hole and buries a person. It can lay to waste an entire life and it takes down anyone who's trying to pull the sufferer out. I had to decide whether I wanted to follow my husband, fall into this hole and be buried with him, or look after my own life and find a better path for me and my child.

I so wanted to be free. I didn't want to waste my life, and our relationship was worn out. But how could I get away and leave a such great person and the dad to my daughter? I felt such a lack of power. I couldn't abandon the person who treated my daughter as his own child, and I didn't want to feel guilty. I lacked control and I loved him, so I still wanted to try to make it work. It took another four years of my life.

One day, when I arrived back home after work, I found my husband cooking. We sat down at the table. He knew me so well, he could tell just by looking at me. He said, 'Go on, you can tell me.'

'I can't do it anymore. I need to go. I am so unhappy,' I said, in tears.

He held my face, with his own tears falling, and said, 'I can see that. I love you so much, even if I do not show you anymore. And my love is so big that, yes, go, you deserve to be happy. I cannot offer you this anymore. It would be too selfish to ask you to stay and waste your life here, looking at this miserable man I've become. You deserve more.

'Please only promise me that we will stay connected. Take your time and when you are ready, stay my friend.'

I made the decision to leave Spain, where we were living at the time. He took me to the airport and, in that moment, when I walked into the terminal to check my luggage, I could not look behind me, because I knew he was standing there in tears. I felt so bad. How could I do that? But inside my heart, I was so frustrated that my only impulse was to get out of that prison. I desperately needed to cross that threshold to my freedom. With a huge weight in my heart and in my steps, I crossed through security to my new life, holding my little girl's hand.

I came to UK to try a new life. My sister lived there. I had no idea how life was going to be. Another country, another language, another challenge to survive. I wasn't sure about anything except that I did not want to live the life I had. I could not stay in the same town as my ex. I ran away and I never regretted it.

3

I moved to London in 2009, full of expectations, with very basic English, and got my first job as a nanny. About two months after my arrival, a friend and I went to a club. We were dancing and three Brazilian guys joined us. My friend knew one of them. They were funny and we shared lots of drinks. Two of them were cute and they were discussing who could kiss my friend.

The third one was less cute, and he was sweating. His T-shirt was so wet. He said to me, 'While my friends do the *duello* over who is going to flirt with your friend and have her kiss them as a reward, why don't you give me your phone number, so I can call you? I'm already too drunk to try anything with you today.'

Oh, dear. He was so funny, but not a good flirt, I thought, but I gave him my number, anyway. So he was happy, but I thought that he had no chance with me as we kept dancing.

Two days after that, he called me. 'You were very drunk so I thought you had lost my number,' I said. He replied, 'Even if I had passed out, I would keep it safe in my pocket.'

We ended up going for a drink in a pub and I saw him in a much better light, not sweating, not drunk and much nicer, but with the same friendliness. And he made me laugh, so it was a great evening. After ten years, I ended up having my first kiss from someone other than my ex-husband.

I still remember his hands holding me, making me feel so warm and desirable. I could feel how hard he was while he hugged me tight. It had been a while since I had a deep French kiss. His tongue made me feel how hungry he was for me. How nice is the feeling of someone wanting you?

There was a fiery spark between us that lasted for two years. We never had a serious relationship, but I was hooked on him. Then one day we had a small, jealous discussion because he'd let me down, and we spent few days not talking to each other. One afternoon, I got a message from his friend:

Hey, what are you doing? We are in a pub. Fancy joining us?

Yes, I can be with you guys in forty minutes, I answered, feeling excited to see him.

I arrived and he was sitting with the friend who texted me. There was another girl beside him and he gave her a kiss just when I spotted them.

I approached the table and asked them, 'Is that why you told me to join you both? To punish me? For what?!' And I left, feeling so angry.

Later I played the same silly game, paying him back by going out with another guy, and then we separated.

A few months after, I was out with my girlfriends and he phoned me. It was 1:00 a.m.

'What are you up to?' he asked me.

'I am out in Clapham with friends, but I'm going home now. The club is closing. We are going to keep drinking at my house. My daughter is sleeping over at her friend's.'

'We are out, too. Can we join you girls?' he asked.

'Yes, sure,' I replied. I had butterflies in my belly. I was looking forward to seeing him.

My friends and I went home and, half an hour later, he arrived with his group. He was very drunk.

He held me and tried to kiss me, but he was very rough and breathing alcohol. 'I miss you,' he said. 'You have another guy, don't you?'

'You are drunk. What else did you have tonight?'

He took me to my bedroom, and he locked the door.

He put me on the bed and started to squeeze my body, my breasts, and trying to kiss me.

'You are hurting me,' I shouted at him, but he just ignored this, taking my clothes off and fucking me. The only thing he said was, 'You are mine.'

This was not the way I wanted us to reconnect. I felt so angry that I stayed quiet, waiting for him to finish and looking in his face, wanting him to look me in the eye, but he avoided that until after. I touched my pussy, putting some of his cum on my hand to show him, and I shouted, 'You have finished, so get out of my house!'

He looked at me and was about to say something when I shouted again. 'Get out! You should be more romantic to get what you want.'

He left.

He spent all week texting me, without any reply.

I am so sorry. I was so drunk and more. Don't be angry. Please.

Please answer my phone calls.

If you don't talk to me, I will come to your house. Don't kill me.

That was his last message. I was not angry at him, but I wanted to punish him. He couldn't just talk to me after doing what he did. He needed to change his behaviour.

Two days after that, at 2:00 a.m., my phone rang. It was his flatmate. I didn't answer, but he persisted many times, so I answered the phone.

'He was very drunk when he took his motorbike and left. Is he with you?' he asked me.

'No, he's not here,' I answered and put down the phone.

Thirty minutes later, the phone rang again. 'Come here. The police are here. He fell off his motorbike. He is dead.'

My body felt like it shattered into pieces. *Is this a bad joke?* He must have been trying to get attention. It couldn't be possible.

'Don't joke like that. It's not funny,' I said, struggling to speak.

'It is not a joke.'

I grabbed my keys and drove to his house. On the way, I saw the road was closed and police were everywhere. No one could cross the tape. The body had already been removed, as it was a fatal accident, but that was when I spotted his motorbike, destroyed. And my heart was destroyed, too.

I went with his mum and his brother to his funeral, as I needed support to get inside. They went first, while I stayed outside composing myself. I didn't want to see him. I heard his mum screaming and crying and I was not ready.

After a while, I decided to go in. He was there, sleeping forever, and I couldn't cry. I struggled to breathe. I only held his face, kissed his lips and whispered in his ear, 'I wasn't angry with you. I am so sorry.'

I spent a long time feeling guilty, thinking I would never fall in love with anyone again. My emotions shut down and I entered a phase of going out with different men every weekend. I even started to take substances to get through the nights of clubbing.

But time heals all wounds, and the scars that were left helped me to become a stronger woman.

When death separates people who are connected, it leaves doubts about what is beyond. Most people believe in God and are linked to some religion; where one believes in paradise, others believe in being reunited after death or in reincarnation. I don't believe any of it though. I believe in existence and extinction. I don't believe in anything after death and it motivates me not to cling to the past, as what is gone is gone. So even if my heart still felt pain, my brain wanted to move on and make my existence worthwhile before my own extinction. This gave me the motivation to not be attached to the past, to make changes in my life, because if I do not have a tomorrow, my existence ends and so does my story. I do not want a life full of tears or monotony.

It had been four years since the loss of my friend and I was looking in the mirror. I saw myself, age forty-five. Wrinkles had begun to appear and there were some strands of grey hair. The years had passed and here I still was, in a boring life and still struggling with money. Sexually? I was completely frustrated, still hanging out with a few guys and not finding anyone interesting or gaining anything.

I had my body and boobs enhanced then, and my self-esteem rose a lot, but I felt like time was running out too quickly. I wanted to make my life more exciting. After all those one-night stands, I still didn't really meet anyone nice, anyone who touched my feelings or who wanted more than to just empty their balls; and I wanted quality sex. I felt as if I was just a tray of food to serve and feed men whenever they were hungry, and I did it for free.

After almost 5 years working in catering, my daughter was 17 years old, I didn't have a job. But I was good-looking for my age – a real MILF (I never liked to be called MILF though).

I had a few dreams, such as maybe going back to studying, getting a better job or travelling, but my age was what it was and I had no qualifications. How long would I be on this road? It made me laugh when I heard the saying 'Age is just a number.'

This number does not stop rising and it is merciless. I needed money quickly and I was wondering if it was worthwhile to keep hanging out with men from dating sites when so many were of them were married. I was carrying on, just surviving, feeling sorry for myself, crying about all my bad experiences. I had to do something to make a change, to stop the struggle to the end of the month. My life felt so empty. Serving tables in a restaurant would never take me any further.

I don't play the lottery, but getting a rich man is the dream of many women. But this thought never convinced me. I can sell my time and my body, but I could never sell my freedom. I won't sleep every night in the same bed with someone I don't love. I am too wild for that. I want to ensure that when I get older, I do not need to depend on any man financially, as, at this point in my life, I have decided to keep myself free. And I am happy

4

After my divorce and the loss of my friend, I felt too drained to give myself to someone else, but I was strong enough to start again. And this is what I wanted: more money to do what I loved most. To be free and travel. I needed to earn money fast to do this.

'I need to find a job. I am so tired of taking CVs everywhere, then feeling extremely disappointed and tired from not getting anywhere. Plus, my bills are overdue. The answer is always the same: I will let you know,' I said to my friend, who does massage, when I entered her studio.

'I also had this guy who said that my CV didn't have much experience. I told him I spent a long time doing the same job; perhaps that means I am a reliable person.'

'Lie down here and I will give you a massage to relax,' my friend told me, pushing me onto the massage table.

Oh dear, how good I felt, my body relaxing, her oiled hands touching my back.

'You are nice looking and have a nice body,' she said. 'You look ten years younger than your age. Why you don't you start escorting for a temporary period, just until you resolve your money situation?'

At that point, I was already lost in her hands. My body was so relaxed, so I said, 'You know what, that might be a good idea. Do you know anyone who can help me?'

'Yes, I do. I will sort it out for you.'

It was Friday night, April 2015; I was at home with no plans to go out when my phone rang.

'Hi, I am Fernanda, my masseuse gave me your number. I need a girl to make up a foursome. Wanna join us?'

'Yes,' I said immediately, as I needed some cash. I dressed myself and quickly did my make-up. Within twenty minutes I was on my Lambretta, heading across to her house.

'Don't die on me. This is my chance!' I shouted at my phone, as the battery died and I lost the GPS. I needed to find the address.

I was almost an hour late when I arrived, and I was sweating.

Should I try or just go back? I thought about leaving, but I needed my phone to get home anyway. The booking had probably already finished, but I still wanted to meet with and apologise to Fernanda, as she still could be helpful in terms of getting my start in all this. I decided I would talk to her and ask if I could charge my phone.

I rang the doorbell and a blonde lady answered. 'Hi, I'm Lily. I am so sorry, my phone died and I couldn't find the flat, so I had to ask around.'

'Hey, come in, the party will take all night,' she replied, turning to the guys. 'She has arrived.'

I went inside and they greeted me and, unexpectedly, I didn't feel too nervous, only a bit shy, but relieved to still have my chance to do this date. I was feeling grateful that what Fernanda offered would pay a few of my overdue bills.

The clients were already very high on cocaine. Fernanda sat in the middle of them, took a line and invited me to join her. It was not my first time sniffing coke, so I accepted. I figured it would help me to stay up all night and make me more relaxed.

'I need a shower,' I said and one of the guys asked me, 'Can I join you?'

I smiled and he followed me to the shower room. Nothing could make him hard though. He went down on me, almost desperately, but his cock was not responding.

With all the lines on the table, even Viagra would not be helpful. The guys finally left around dawn, and when Fernanda and I woke up, she started laughing.

'You passed the test. They loved you. You are hot, they said, so we need a profile for you.'

'They were off their heads, so of course they liked me,' I answered, both of us laughing now.

'I will make you a profile,' she said.

So, for the first time in my life, I exchanged sex for money.

Fernanda was very cheerful and sympathetic. We got along well and she introduced me to this new world, inviting me to work at her flat where, sometimes, she had couple of other girls on weekends, so her clients would have more choice. She took forty percent of whatever we made. I used a room in her house, free of charge, so I only needed to buy my personal stuff, like outfits, condoms, lube and so on.

Fernanda had a big heart. Bigger than what she herself could imagine. She was not selfish and that was probably why, so many times, I saw people taking advantage of her. She was too soft when we talked about men and their lack of affection. I used to tell her all the time that if a man is not able to respect her job, he has no right to reap the benefits from it.

Lee makes website profiles for foreigners and charges for it. I didn't want to pay, so I decided to make my own profile. Thus, in the website called AdultWork, 'Felicity' was born – it's an ordinary name, but I didn't have much choice, as all the names I wanted were already taken. For the neighbourhood where we were, it was enough to start me off. I just needed a nice naked picture. It was not difficult.

Francisco, a Colombian guy, came in one afternoon, looking for just a bit of sex. He left with a big smile on his face. He enjoyed my silicone, and that night he called me again, asking me to come to his flat, because it was his friend's birthday and he wanted me to be his gift.

I dressed in my latex trousers and a red top showing half of my breasts, with nice lingerie and a motorbike jacket. I took my helmet and went on my Lambretta to my first outcall.

I arrived and all the guys stared at me, wondering what the hell was going on.

So, I started the scenario.

'Who is the birthday boy?'

'Me!' a guy sitting in a chair answered.

'Happy birthday. I am your gift. Come and unwrap it.' And then I took off my jacket, with all of them staring at my cleavage popping out of the sexy lingerie underneath.

'Francisco, put on some music, please,' I told his friend.

Then I took his belt off, unzipped his trousers and started to do a striptease. Dancing and undressing myself slowly to the rhythm of the music, I rubbed his face between my tits and my arse. Everyone laughed a lot, but the atmosphere started to warm up.

I took him to a corner and fucked him right there. My time ended, but Francisco wanted to fuck me too.

I said, 'Let's do a quick one.' Then I left.

I worked for a few more days and then I got a message on my phone from the website, asking me to follow a link. It was spam and I had my profile stolen. It's apparently quite common on this website, which was not run by an agency. You needed to deal with your profile yourself.

But no profile means no money. So disappointing.

Without a profile on an escort website, my only option was to try dating websites, and, this time, I needed to focus not on the young and handsome or businessmen looking to have a fuck. It was easier going to middle-aged men, who are average looking or retired. Those are easier to convince to give you money. After a few chats and going for drinks, when they started to try to go deeper, I asked for money. A few guys did not take this very nicely and let me down, but I also had some who accepted paying.

I met Ge, a delightful person who was around sixty-five. He invited me to go to his house near the beach and spend the night with him. I got straight to the point and he understood, offering me an amount of money for an overnight. This was a girlfriend experience, where we go to dinner, have a few drinks and, after, go to his home.

However, he was impotent sexually due to major depression caused by the loss of his two children, both to overdoses. He was currently looking to regain his sexual appetite. It was already too late, though; we met twice and did not have sex.

'He is cute,' I thought when I got a message from Jim. 'But he is not gonna accept paying. He is a baby,' I told myself, while I scrolled through his pictures and read that he was only twenty-one years old. He persisted with the messages though, and I responded, but there was no way I was going to fuck such a young guy. For that reason, at the beginning, I was making it difficult for us to meet up. But he sounded nice, so sweet and polite and with a radiant smile; his lips made me want to eat him whole. So, in the end, I told him that I was an escort and I charged for sex, and then I received the sweetest response a person could ever give to me:

Oh, Lily, I already realised that I should start saving money because I really would love to see you.

He worked in a council office and I needed to send an email, so he offered to help me with some paperwork, English spelling, whatever, and it was the perfect excuse to have him come to my house without me feeling any guilt.

After exchanging glances and provocative smiles, we finished the work and then we kissed. I began to caress him everywhere, kissing his neck and touching his body and 'down there'. I started to take off his pants, but I realised he had an orgasm before I even finished undressing him. His pants were soaked as he could not stand it. His face was red because his jeans were wet, but he was so sweet that I tried to soothe him, saying, 'Don't worry. It happens.'

'This is the problem. I cum so quickly. I cannot hold it in. I cannot go to a girl and do this. It is so embarrassing. I need a more experienced person to help me.'

I smiled at him. 'I will enjoy being useful, but definitely, you need to learn to hold things in.' Jim then became my toy boy for two years.

5

Nobody knows what I am doing. I haven't told anyone, but I go to see my sister at her house and I want to tell her what I am doing. She was the only person who I wanted to know; I trusted her.

We were sitting on the sofa when I said it.

'I am selling sex. I don't have a job and I decided to do it for a while until I can fix my money situation.'

She stared at me; I saw tears forming in her eyes.

'For God's sake, don't do this! Things will resolve themselves and this is not the way to fix your problems.'

But I am determined and she knows that just by looking at me.

'OK,' she said at last, 'I will never agree with you doing this, but please, be careful.'

'I will. I need you to have my work number. When I go to visit a client, I will send you the address and time that I will be there. I am afraid too, but I want to do it. I need to change my life.'

Before I made another profile, I kept trying the dates websites to try to make extra cash. Fernanda brought clients to me and I ended up with a bit of cash in my pocket after handing over her forty percent.

One night, she told me she was going to introduce me to James.

She sent him a text: *James, I have a new friend that you will like.*

He asks for a picture and, later, turns up at Fernanda's estate in a cab.

Tall, young, very well-dressed, he was a banker who lived in Canary Wharf. And he also had a big cock. I sighed. *Finally, an exciting man.*

I felt attracted to him. He liked cocaine, We had lot of fun that night. We did about three grams and he stayed at the flat, as we were very high. In the morning, I wanted to have a little time alone with him. I made a coffee for us and took it to my room. Fernanda did not like this very much, but I wanted to have an orgasm and he was so nice and handsome. We were still high. *Oh, James. How hot you are.*

Fernanda did not do outcalls, so when a guy wanted her to go to his hotel, she asked if she could take me along, too. He accepted.

She negotiated the price for us both and we went. It was my first time seeing a client in Central London. We drank with him, got a little tipsy, and after, in a cab on the way back, crossing Tower Bridge, we contemplated the beauty of the London night. We were like two little girls, laughing, hugging each other, celebrating our friendship.

'How I love this view. It is so powerful to feel like part of this city.' I whispered, looking at it all passing by the window.

Every day was a party in that flat. Fernanda was always smiling. She was a delight and a great madam, if what she was doing could be called that, as in the UK, what she was doing was illegal, considered exploitation. One night, she told me, 'There is someone who wants to be whipped. This is with you.'

I freaked out. 'What?!'

'I will be in the room with you,' she said.

He arrived with his nose already full of drugs. I threw him on the floor.

'Have you been a naughty boy and need to be punished? On your knees!' I ordered him.

'Do you want me to beat you?' He said he did, so I started slapping his face and beating him with my cane. 'You want more?'

'Yes.'

I put the tip of my high heel in his mouth and made him suck it. 'Kiss my foot!' And then I beat him some more. My arms were already aching, so I told him to leave. But not much later, he came back wanting more.

My arms could not take anymore. His skin was already marked and almost bleeding.

I could barely sleep that night, wondering how someone could enjoy that kind of thing. How could I do that to someone? I was in shock, but I had a strange feeling of satisfaction, mixed with guilt.

I met another guy on a dating website who agreed to pay me. I went to a hotel to meet him. He took a large dose of Viagra because the bastard was determined to fuck my arse for all three hours without any break.

I always liked anal sex, and, at the beginning, it was very pleasurable. He was good looking and had a great physique. But he was a low type of person, who thought, 'I'm going to pay and then I'm going to do damage.'

I spent three weeks after that meeting not being able to walk straight. I went to the doctor, thinking that I needed treatment. He laughed, already guessing what had happened. He said, 'Your anus is the strongest muscle of your body. If you go to the gym occasionally, your muscle aches, but if you go constantly, your muscles get tight.' He advised me to rest and use some cold compresses, and said that in a few more days I would feel better.

I realised I urgently needed a profile. This situation was not right. Being someone's bitch and poor was not a good combination. I've got to start making some real money, I thought.

The question was, how could I make myself stand out?

I did not want to be an ordinary prostitute, to just open my legs for money and wait for my clients to cum. Or to be babysitting guys full of coke.

In any industry, a job is only done well if it is done with pleasure. What do I like sexually?

Then a certain man came to my mind; he was my inspiration.

Mr Difficult was one of the guys I met through a dating website before I started to ask for money. When I was doing it just for fun. He was another one who wanted me just like a tray of free food when he was hungry, but he left me impressed in that at least he worked to give me exciting experiences, and he put effort into it. Until our first meeting, sex was basic and the kinkiest thing for me was to do blow jobs and anal. And give some pats on the arse, of course.

It was thus impossible to forget him.

Before we met, I had gotten tired of going out with guys just to fuck, so it had been about three months since I'd had sex. I decided to reply to his message and, after a few chats, we agreed to see each other. I just wanted to get laid, because I had stopped hanging out and clubbing and had been alone for a long time.

He ended up cancelling because of the rain and, sounding a little arrogant, said that it would not be possible to fuck me on the bonnet of his Aston Martin due to the weather.

I had no idea what an Aston Martin was.

'Doesn't matter, come to my flat. I am alone tonight, we can have some fun,' I answered.

'You seem a little suspicious to me,' he said.

'What?' I got very irritated. 'Why do I look suspicious?' *Who does he think he is?* I thought.

Then I just left the chat and, two days later, he sent me a message apologising. Still, I was a bit annoyed, so I got straight to the point:

Look, Mr Difficult, the thing is, it's been over three months without me having sex. What is your problem? If you do not want to come over to fuck me, just leave it. I will try another guy.

He did not expect this answer from me, I guess. Because in about an hour, I heard the sound of a loud car pulling up outside the front of my flat. I watched from the window as he got out of his sports car. He approached my door and knocked, and that is when I found out what an Aston Martin was.

6

Mr Difficult was handsome, blonde and a little bald. I find bald men very charming. He was not exactly my type, but he was attractive enough and suited to the purpose. He was a bit snobby and talked in a posh voice.

He said, 'I don't have much time. I can't stay for long.'

When we were both naked, he grabbed my hair, directing my mouth to his penis. 'I like a woman on her knees and to suck me until she chokes,' he told me.

'Slowly, deeper,' he asked me, manipulating my head with his hands still in my hair. I felt a warmth down there and got super wet, feeling an uncontrollable desire for him to penetrate me. He was about to cum and pulled my hair, taking his cock out of my mouth. He then threw me on the bed and started to lick me.

My libido was very high and I could not stand it. I screamed while having an intense orgasm with him penetrating me and he also came hard, leaving me completely soaked.

We talked for a bit. He was relaxing on the bed with my head on his lap. I was surprised that he stroked my hair, which I found comforting. After a while, he was ready for a second round. I sighed when he left my house.

Mr Difficult liked messaging to talk slutty. He also liked to make sure all selfies and nudes were taken at the moment and not sent from a phone file, so he would ask for photos with a certain finger on a certain part of the body. He used to ask me questions and use sexual terms that I had no idea about.

I felt very naïve and he enjoyed it. For him, it seemed like sex was all about role playing.

Have you already tried water sports?' he asked me.

'Well, when I was in Australia, I had sex in the sea,' I answered, and he laughed hysterically.

'What about a threesome?' I did not know about that either.

'Another woman?' he asked.

'Makes me sick. Never,' I said.

'I like two girls. I will bring one for you and you will lick her pussy for me. (That annoyed me, as he was not asking, but just imposing what he wanted on me.)

He disappeared for few days, and then I received a message.

What are you doing now?

I just left work and I am on my way home.

I'll be at your house in thirty minutes.

And, again, he did not even ask if he could come – so bossy. But I accelerated on my Lambretta to get home and ran to the shower. I felt excited to see him again.

I gasped when I opened the door. He was dressed in an impeccable suit and, despite the tired expression in his eyes, was dazzlingly hot.

'Why are you dressed like that?'

'I just got back from a seminar in Paris. I'm stressed.'

'Then come in, let's relax.'

He chuckled while we entered my flat. I went to give him a kiss but he held me back and smiled, saying, 'I already told you that I like you on your knees, sucking me.'

I laughed and got on my knees, wondering to myself if he was always like this. I tried to caress his bottom but he said, 'No, no, naughty girl, put your hands behind you or I'll have to tie them.'

'Don't. I have a phobia,' I said, but I was enjoying the role play. I'd never done it and, again, my hands wanted to touch him, but he took them off.

'I already told you to keep your hands behind you, naughty,' he said, and slapped my bottom.

When I tried to touch him for the fortieth time, he threw me on the bed, pulling my arms up over my head and holding them with one of his hands, while using the other to hold his cock and very roughly penetrate me, fucking me very hard without letting me touch him. It was an indescribably pleasurable feeling.

After, lying down like we did the first time, with me leaning between his legs, he asked me:

'Did you like it?'

'Very much. I am afraid of being tied up, but that is probably why it makes me horny.'

'Sometimes what we are afraid of is what makes us excited. Do you know what a dungeon is?'

I didn't.

He took his phone and started showing me pictures of him fucking a girl in a dungeon.

She had duct tape over her eyes and her hands were tied up with it. Completely immobilised, she was sucking him, completely helpless, unable to see him. The picture imprinted on my mind, excited me.

'I want to go to this place. Would you take me?' I asked him.

'I like to be bossy, but I'm not very into bondage and pain. Maybe one day. It is not about domination; it is about trust. You should make a list of things that you haven't done, then tick which ones you would like to try and which you wouldn't do.'

On Sunday, I got a message from him around 8:00 p.m.

I want a threesome. Want to see you licking a woman.

What?

You said you never tried a girl; so, I want you to do it.

Where are you?

At the cinema, waiting for our girl.

Oh my God, my blood was boiling. I did not understand why he liked to hurt me. He sent me a picture of her. She was stunning and young. I was hysterically jealous.

You are an idiotic bastard for sending me a picture of a girl at the cinema with you.

She will be yours.

Oh, really? Really for me, or for you?

For us.

I don't know if you are funny or ridiculous.

And then he went quiet. This was the most ridiculous thing he had said to me so far, and it hurt me. I was jealous.

Jealous of a man who I had seen just few times, who liked to do all these funny domination role plays and could leave me unable to sleep all night. I didn't even know his full name; he was just Mr Difficult.

There were no more messages. Being a drama queen and revealing my jealousy did not work with him.

It was week before I was leaving on a long trip to see my family, and I had to have my Lambretta checked. I was on my way to pick it up when I got a text from him.

Even while I was deciding whether to tell him to fuck off, I couldn't stop myself from smiling.

Where are you?

On the bus on my way to pick up my Lambretta from the mechanic.

I want to see you. Do me a selfie.

So, I did one. *Happy?* I asked, sarcastically.

When you get the station, I want you to go into a lingerie shop; pick up something nice and go to the fitting room. I want another selfie of you wearing it. I am horny.

So was this guy crazy, or was I not well, I wondered to myself. While I felt tired of his games, I couldn't say no to him, and I kind of liked it. I never thought I would ever do things like this, but here I was.

When are you free?

Today.

I will come to see you.

Oh, finally, I thought.

But I have a parents' meeting at my daughter's school in the evening.

No problem. We can meet after.

This was an improvement. It was nice to see him persisting, instead of being difficult and bossy.

But then, a few hours later, there arrives another text:

Great. See you later. We are having a threesome. I will bring your girl for you.

What? I went into shock.

I told you. I want you to try a girl. You will do it tonight. Don't you want that?

I'm not sure. Give me time to make up my mind.

I want you to do it. And it is happening tonight.

I spent all day thinking about it. I felt so nervous and did not tell him that I bought one of the lingerie sets from the selfie.

I texted a friend saying I had a date and she giggled, telling me to send my daughter to her house. I arrived home, tided everything quickly and lit candles to create an inviting atmosphere. I then put on the lingerie and waited for his arrival, with her.

I opened the door and was ecstatic. She was so beautiful, even more so than in the picture. I still wasn't sure if I could do it, though. She looked like an angel and was so young. But I am not the kind of woman to back down or show that I'm feeling inferior, even though I felt insecure all the time with him.

I could not compete with her, so, I thought, let's just play. Despite being so young, she took the lead very quickly as he stroked her legs gently and took off her shoes, treating her like a princess. I stood still, not showing how I felt, which was extremely jealous. He never did that to me. But soon, she turned to me and started kissing me. My heart was beating so fast and I felt like I'd lost my mind. I was confused. He was watching us kissing with a very satisfied expression.

I had never kissed a woman before. I felt the warmth of her lips and the softness of her tongue and it started to make me warm. He then fucked me while I was licking her. Her juice was so sweet and her pussy so gorgeous. That was what he wanted, to see me doing that for the first time. Then he reversed to fuck her, also in doggie style, while she licked me. Our eyes met and he looked at me sarcastically and I whispered to him, 'You are a bastard.'

He giggled, making a smug face.

When we finished, he gave her money for a cab. I asked her to stay all night, but she left anyway.

He laid on the bed and looked at me, smiling. 'You bought the lingerie, but not the one I liked most.'

'It was too expensive. I couldn't afford that,' I told him.

'Silly woman. I would have helped you to buy it. By the way, did you enjoy tonight?'

I patted his shoulder, saying, 'You are naughty,' and he laughed.

He kissed me. 'Now there is only you and me. Let's play more. You didn't cum.'

'Finally! Let's do it. I was too nervous before.' It was nice to feel his hands holding me.

That was the last time I saw him before I went on the long holiday with my family. He came to see me the day I got back, but then he left the UK to work abroad.

7

I contacted Lee, the man who wrote profiles for girls and charged for it. He was very clever, so he helped me to understand the terms and conditions of the website I had chosen, AdultWork. It is the most powerful site on this industry. He knew the right words to use, and he gave me all the tips to avoid spam and having my profile stolen again. Certainly, it would have been simple for an English woman, but it was not easy for a foreigner, as my English was not great.

I took a trip to Paris while waiting for the site verification.

When I was visiting the Eiffel Tower, my phone buzzed with his message: *Break out the champagne. You are now Lily Lashes.*

Fernanda accepted my offer of money to use her flat, instead of sharing my income. I wanted my own room. I spoke much better English than her and the other girls were not making much money and were undocumented, so she felt safer with me, and the money I offered was good. She was an easy-going person; we were close friends. But I wanted to have my own clients. I was starting to be busy and I wanted to be free to choose my schedule and my clients, and to spend more time at home with my daughter. I didn't like the idea of having a schedule, as I felt like a shop with opening and closing times, and I didn't want to see people who used drugs.

I was looking for longer bookings, as I felt that was much more enjoyable than having a guy who comes just for a quick fuck. I wanted to feel like an escort, not a prostitute.

What is the difference, you might say, when the product on sale is the same? It is the difference between a guy who is there for fifteen minutes, and you lube your pussy and put his cock into it, just to empty his balls, with not even time for a shower. Versus when you have time to talk for a bit with a polite person, to enjoy yourselves and have fun, doing role play and having a drink together. Those are the things that make the difference in how I feel about the act.

Finally, I got my first booking with my new profile and went to meet wise1safe at a coffee shop in order to go to a naturist spa.

The place was not elegant, but it wasn't unpleasant. It had a sauna, Jacuzzi and a few little rooms to have a fuck. We were having a meal, sitting at the bar, when Ash joined us. She was a hermaphrodite.

We finished the meal and went to a private room where there was a small bed covered with vinyl – easy to clean. A minute after that, someone knocked on the door, meaning that they were asking if they could join us, but the client said no. There were condoms, lube and tissues, but we didn't need them as wise1safe had brought everything we needed. He unpacked his stuff and held out some gloves as he asked Ash to help me fist him; they already knew each other well.

Ash and I exchanged numbers, and a week later, I got a message from her, asking me to pay her a visit to her boyfriend.

I had a tattoo session in the afternoon and when I finished, I made my way to her house.

Ash was born with both sex organs and has an entirely tattooed body. She had a big cock, but under her balls was her pussy. Inside that rare body lived a completely feminine, lovely and very adorable, sensitive woman. She was so sweet, and never made me feel awkward or uncomfortable from the first moment I met her.

When I arrived at her flat, I saw a very sad expression on her face, which cut off my excitement. She was doing this for her partner, who was very excited. She gave me an envelope with my gift and offered me a drink. I accepted and she went to the kitchen to prepare the drink, leaving me alone with her boyfriend.

I think she didn't want to watch the meeting. He began to caress me, adoring my intimate parts. He then put on a condom and finished in just a few minutes.

She came in crying. She seemed very disillusioned. I did not want to imagine what was going on in her mind.

She got down on her knees, trying to suck him, but he was done. I tried to kiss her, but she spun around and soon was on her knees beside me, giving me a strong hug.

I felt so bad. I whispered into her ear, 'Do want me to leave?'

She said, 'Yes, please.'

I got dressed and left the house.

I messaged her several times after that, but she never answered me. That tightens my heart because, many years after, I met a guy who said that he also knew her. He had read on some punter's blog that she took her life. I really hope this was a fake rumour. Ash never left my thoughts, but I did so much Google research and never found anything about her.

I finally got a message from Mr Difficult about when he would arrive in London.

Landed today. How's escorting going?

It is OK. Started getting my clients. Have a nice flat in Peckham.

Where is it? Are you with your friend?

Yes. Want to come?

Can I see you both of you now? Selfie, please.

We are in pyjamas.

Good. Don't be shy, girls.

I send him a selfie of us.

Now, who has the biggest breasts?

You are so naughty. I do.

Prove it. Both PJ tops off.

No. You come and check.

You are too shy. I am one mile from you. Haven't picked up my car yet. I will run down there and will need a shower when I arrive. Be there in thirty min. You two girls get dressed for me.

You are always so bossy. Do this, do that ...

You don't like it?

I do. (I really do like him.)

He arrived dressed in shorts and a Regatta top, and he was so sweaty. I opened the door and felt the same butterflies in my belly as all the other times I'd seen him. He was so handsome. And he had changed his look. He was completely bald now and it made him even sexier. I was so attracted to him. I threw myself in his arms.

'I missed you. I can't believe you are back.' He went to shower and then

I took him to my room and started taking off the towel around his waist.

He stopped me, and started giving orders. 'Calm down. Did you forget how I like you? On your knees, sucking me and looking straight into my eyes.'

Then he sat on the bed, with me on my knees as I started to suck.

'Where is your friend?' he asked me. 'Let's enjoy her.' And then Fernanda joined us.

He fucked me, watching me playing with her. The day after, I messaged him.

Did you get your car? Please, send me the pics you took of us.

Yes. All good. (I receive the pics.)

OMG ... I shouldn't do that.

Do what?

The pics. But I'm happy I did it. I will remember that.

Why? You're not seeing me again?

Of course, I will. But you are too difficult.

Then, he sent me pic of another girl.

She is the next one.

Have you been with her?

Not fucked. Just sucking, years ago. We are playing on Thursday, daytime.

Do you like her?

She is fun. Haven't seen her in ages. More than a year.

Why don't you see her alone? You are really obsessed by threesomes.

I want to see you sucking her. I want you.

You want me just for your threesome. You don't come to see me alone anymore, like when we first met.

Don't have a little moment.

Excuses and excuses.

I opened the door and saw this very stylish girl. He had good taste in women. Let's go straight to the action then, as that was all he wanted. I ate her pussy while he fucked me from behind. He didn't go down on her. I think I also enjoyed girls at that point and it was what he wanted. He wanted me, but he was turned on by seeing me having other girls. Only then did I understand why he told me that first time when he was at the cinema with another girl. He wanted me to play; it turns him on.

He left just after he finished playing with us. She stayed a bit longer and told me a few things about him. I asked her if he was always like that, so strange.

'Not strange, just it's his thing. But he is a very reserved person. I liked him a few years ago and really tried to make something happen between us, but nothing did.'

I texted him the day after.

I had a dream about you. Take me to the dungeon; only you and me. Want you to tie me up and whip me. It is a good place to challenge myself. I would like to see if I could trust completely in someone. I have issues about trusting people. I am not asking you to have me has your woman or girlfriend. Just asking you to challenge my trust. I really want to do it with you.

Bondage and pain are not my thing, but let's check the availability.

So, are you gonna do what I want?

Isn't it supposed to be the other way around? If I am in charge, then you do what I want. And I want you while you play with a woman.

It is the only thing I've asked for since I met you. I've done everything you wanted.

OK, let's book it then.

I tried to book it, but sadly it was fully booked and I was very disappointed.

I went to get a tattoo, and while I was in pain, I sent him a pic.

Who is that?

Me.

When did you decide to do that?

A while ago. It is so painful. Trying to distract myself.

Think of my cum shooting over your face.

Hmm ... facial treatment. Nice.

When do you want this facial?

Thursday is good for me.

Good. Thursday morning. I want to fuck your ass. You complain I never do what you like. And it will be only you and me.

I've been wanting it for so long.

Then you will have it.

He arrived and, again, left after a very short time. At least the play was between only him and me. I felt satisfied, but when he said he was going out to meet his friend, I felt very disappointed. I wanted him to spend time with me.

That was my only quick moment on my own with him. We didn't stay in bed after sex caressing and talking anymore. He was now living overseas and, when he came to the UK, I never met up with him. We sometimes exchanged texts, but I never saw him again. I felt sad for a long time because I wasn't his toy girl anymore. I was starting to enjoy the role play and my fun was gone.

8

The way I worked was changing. I was meeting so many clients, many of whom enjoyed BDSM both ways. I put this service on my profile, as I was very interested in exploring this fetish and pushing my boundaries. I started to visit sex shops and watched lots of porn movies about it. It turned me on.

Beast was very sexy guy who wanted to play at domination.

He tied me up, got my leather whip and started to hit my back. It was made of soft leather, so it made noise but was not very painful. I started to discover new sexual desires.

While I was being whipped, Mr Difficult would very often come into my mind, even though bondage and whips were not his thing.

Beast had strong hands and a strong attitude. He finished up by using my collar, tying me up while I was on all fours. He had an orgasm with a groan of great satisfaction, while I was on the bed, completely immobilised.

Serious bondage play is about domination, possession, selfishness, and the challenge of trust, submission and being under the control of someone else. It could be done with your man, or just someone who will take you to be used. It is hard to explain because, for me, it was also a new feeling. I was hoping to have this experience with Mr Difficult, but it only happened with clients, so it didn't make me emotionally satisfied.

I was now offering domination services, but more dominant than submissive. Inside, I was hoping for my Alpha. I kept doing role play while I waited to find him.

A guy wanted to be humiliated, so I prepared a scenario.

I opened the door, screaming and telling him off.

'You are late!'

'I finished work late.'

'Where's my money?'

'It's in my pocket.'

I took the money and threw it in his face.

'Is that all you brought? You are useless. Go and get me a glass of water.'

When he gave me the glass, I hit his hand, pouring water all over him. 'It's not cold. I want it with ice.' He came back with another glass of ice water.

I took a sip and said, 'You made me very nervous waiting for you.'

I threw him on his knees in front of me and slapped him in the face. 'I do not like to wait. Now the only way I'll calm down is if I cum. You'd better lick me very well. Otherwise, you will have to go begging in the street to bring me more money.'

I grabbed him, pulling his hair, and then lowered my panties and sat on the bed with my legs open, making him lick my holes.

'Lick my arse and lick it right. Lick like a dog when it is cleaning its plate. You need to deserve the pleasure of satisfying your owner. If I cum nicely, you can fuck me. If I don't, you will wank.' (Asking him to lick me like a dog was the worst thing I ever had to say to someone, as I so love animals!)

A few days later, he told me he had cancer. A few weeks after that, he booked me again, but had to cancel on the day. He was recovering in hospital.

I still think about him. I hope he recovered. He seemed like a good person to me. Meeting this guy made me realise that humiliation was a way to self-punish; it was not my thing. Usually, good or weak people or the frustrated are the ones to seek this kind of service, but it was not for me.

This business is full of crazy people with so many different requests. I had this guy come to see me, very arrogant. He looked at me as if I was a product and said, 'Open your holes as I want to see if you are worth it.'

'Sorry?' I said, already very irritated.

'I will check you first and then I will go to my car to get the money.'

'No, you will go to your car and drive back to your home. Get out of my flat.'

There was a bachelor party, and I was booked to come into a car parts shop. It was already closed when I arrived, and the guys were having drinks inside. I parked my Lambretta just in front of the door, wearing my latex trousers and a sexy top under my jacket.

'Who is the bridegroom?' was my question upon my arrival.

Everybody pointed to this shy guy. I took him to a private corner and removed my clothes. He told me, 'I can't do it. I need to be faithful to my future wife.'

I put my clothes back on, and said, 'Let's pretend we had a great fuck and everybody will be happy.' Then I showed off a bit for the other guys and left.

A chubby Englishman arrived at the apartment, wanting to do fisting. He asked me to be gentle because he had never done it. During the play, he kept his eyes closed and it seemed like he was in a different place. When we finished, I got the urge to ask why he wanted this kind of service and he explained that he cooks cocaine.

'What is that?' I asked him.

He explained that he made cocaine into crack and trafficked it. He had spent two years in jail and, during all that time, when the officers would arrive, he would hide his cell phone inside his anus so that it would not be discovered. Now he wanted to try fisting, thinking that if he got used to it, he could hide drugs while he travelled to sell them.

I was completely speechless. I said goodbye to him, taking him to the door as I gaped.

It was Fernanda's birthday, so we went shopping and stopped at Burger King. While we were sitting there, we saw this black guy arriving in a nice convertible. He walked past our table and Fernanda started flirting him. She loved black men, but was mainly interested in getting clients for her business. He joined us at the table and gave us a ride to her flat.

Fernanda's flat was a penthouse and we sat on the terrace. It was summer and the weather was very nice. During our conversation, he wanted some fun but refused to pay. He was insisting it's wrong to pay for sex. This really annoyed me and Fernanda who was sitting watching us, whispered to me, 'he is a waist of time,' so I asked him, 'What about paying for food?'

I kept on, saying, 'In your country, your brothers don't even have potable water. Your children get stolen to be soldiers. There's so much poverty, just like in my country and others across half of the world, and we do not debate what is shameful. I think we should consider exchanging sex for money as a service like any other.'

'If you had back pain, would you go for a massage?' I continued. 'And if you are hungry, you go to buy food and you pay for it, right? If you don't have money, you don't eat. Is that correct? If you are horny, it is immoral to pay for sex? Why? Well, that is the world we live in, but I won't fuck you if you don't pay me.'

His face was instantly pale; he was speechless. He left the flat but came back a few days later and paid for my service. I am sure he could afford it.

Summertime is very quiet, as people have more choice in terms of going out. My daughter was already sixteen years old and was becoming a young lady. We needed to spend some time together, doing 'ladies' things and so, one day, we spent the afternoon at the hairdresser. My work phone was on silent, but I listed myself as available in case I got a booking. Then I got a call from a guy with a very strange voice.

'You work in Peckham, right? Do you know who I am? If you want to keep working, you better start paying me.'

I just said 'OK' and ended the call.

Then I send him a text:

Hi babe, yeah, I do offer a great service with my strap-on. Also, I offer a bondage and whipping service.

Then I attached a picture with all my cocks.

He called me thirty seconds later. I didn't pick up the phone, and he tried a few more times.

I got scared and called a friend who was in the police. He calmed me down.

'Such threats are not common in this country. It is more likely to be someone wanting to play a joke on you. Give me the number. There are few apps that I can check it on.'

I guess it was. Later, he sent me a message saying that the number was clean. Probably a prank call, as I didn't ever hear from him again.

9

It was a Friday; the phone was quiet. Fernanda and I went for a meal in a Colombian restaurant near Elephant and Castle. She was popular in that area, as she knew many Colombian guys there who used to have brothels or sell drugs.

She was blown away when the waiter came to bring us the menu. 'Thank you,' she replied with a saucy smile. As he left, she looked at me with wide eyes, whispering, 'I like him, he is hot. I wanna fuck him.'

'Yes, he is. A baby. You should take him home,' I replied, smiling.

He had such an angelic and innocent face. He was also very friendly. They started to flirt with each other.

'I have to go back to the flat. My client just texted and made a booking,' I said.

'I am staying,' she told me.

'Good luck, bitch,' I said, laughing as I left.

While I was meeting with my client, I heard noises coming from the flat. It was Fernanda, and she was not alone. The young waiter ended up in her room that night.

I didn't work on weekends, as now I could choose my hours and I preferred to stay home with my daughter. She was leaving soon to spend a month on holiday with my ex-husband. We were still in touch and doing very well as friends, and they really loved each other. I took the advantage of the trip to spend more time at Fernanda's flat and take some extra bookings.

On Monday, when I arrived at the apartment, I saw two huge suitcases in the hallway. I went into Fernanda's room and I spotted them in bed, exchanging caresses, completely in love.

'Are you guys going on holiday?' I asked ironically. She replied, 'He is staying here for a few days until he finds another place to live.'

'So, where are you gonna work?' I asked her.

'Well, we need to share your room for few days, and, as you don't come here every day, I think it will be OK,' she said.

'What about the days I come to work, if we have bookings at the same time?'

'He will need to go downstairs. It's not a problem.'

'It doesn't sound right to me. Seems like we have another pimp here,' I said, but she just ignored me.

A few weeks after, when I arrived to the flat, there was more luggage, and a beautiful girl was in Fernanda's room. They were chatting and laughing loudly.

I went into Fernanda's room and her friend introduced herself: she said her name was Kate. I instantly felt tense.

'What is going on here?' I said. 'This is a house to meet clients, not to party with friends.'

Fernanda replied, 'We are going to work in Brighton tomorrow for a few days.'

I was relieved. They left the next day.

I had a domination booking early one afternoon while they were away. I was late and entered the flat in a rush. The girls had gone but the boy was there, lying on the bed with his friend. They were smoking weed.

'Are you going to work today?' I asked him and he said, 'No, I quit.'

The desire to work wasn't imprinted on his face.

He looked at his friend, smiling, and turned to me, saying, 'Come and have fun with my friend.'

I laughed without saying a word and went to my room.

The client was thirty-one years old but looked younger. He had the flaccid skin of someone who does not exercise much, though. I was shocked by this meeting. After tying him up and whipping him all over his body, he asked me to burst his balls. So, with my high heels, I began to smash his sack. Then I tied up his balls and kneaded them with my shoes until he got hard. Then he asked me to release one of his hands, and he came with a wank. He was probably the guy who impressed me the most. (Well, so far.)

The boy was out and I took my dog to the flat so she wouldn't be home alone. It was a weekend, so I figured I would stay over to make some extra money.

At 11:00 p.m., the phone started to get busy, and the action began.

I got a visit from a guy who wanted anal play done on him, and took some more quick bookings. For a quiet week, that night was busy and, early in the morning, after less than three hours of sleep, I had an outcall booking.

I made it to the client's house. He was full of coke and struggling to get his cock hard. I counted the minutes until I could finish my time and go home, but when I arrived at the flat, someone didn't show up. It was fine, though, because another booking came through.

A Turkish guy arrived. He was very arrogant. I asked for the money.

'I will pay you when I finish.'

I said, already irritated, 'Excuse me? If you don't give me the money now, you can just get out.'

'I am horny, so I will fuck you first and then give you the money.'

It was a nightmare; I was too tired to argue.

'Go home now. I don't want you here.'

'Call your friend. I want to see her. I know there is another girl here.'

'Look, the only thing I'm gonna call for you now is the lift.' I had no more patience. He starts to shout at me. 'Call your friend, now. I am not leaving.'

My body froze. I was starting to get scared as well as annoyed. So, I went to the other room, opened the door and called to my friend. 'Darling, can you come here?'

My dog came in then, wagging her tail, thinking she was going to play. She jumped on him and he was startled, so he leaped up and ran out the door, disappearing in a second. Poor thing. My sweet dog would never bite anyone. I held her close and told her she was a good girl.

It was already midday and we both needed to sleep. Just this once, she deserved a place on the bed.

The girls came back from Brighton. 'I want to talk to you, in private,' Fernanda told me, and we went for a walk to the park.

She started to cry. 'I am not well. The doctors advised me to take a break from work, because it could be cancer. Kate is going to stay with us for a while to help me with money – I need another girl.'

I had a bad feeling about this. I thought she might be lying. The flat only had two bedrooms, and there would be four of us there, including her boyfriend. It seemed like a brothel situation, so I told her, 'You need to get the guy out, so we can have the two rooms for the three of us.'

She said, 'Don't worry, we will resolve this.'

The atmosphere in the house had changed. It was heavy, so I went home early, as my daughter had also come back from her holiday.

After a long shower, I went into my daughter's bedroom, where she was still awake. I got into bed beside her and we had a quick chat.

'Where have you been?' she asked me.

'I was out with friends, but I did not have a good night.' I breathed in deeply, feeling so bad about lying to her. We fell asleep, spooning all night. It was so nice to experience the smell of home.

The next day, when I arrived back at the flat, things got worse. Kate was in my bedroom and Fernanda and her boy were in the other, completely in love.

I went into Fernanda's room, saying, 'This is not what we agreed yesterday. If I must share my room with Kate, I will also share my rent. From today, I will pay half.'

She still was lying down with her boyfriend. She said, 'I need that money.'

It was so annoying. 'And we need both rooms to make that money.'

But they stayed quiet, staring at me, so I left and walked to my room to talk to Kate.

'Look, it's nothing personal. You seem like a nice girl, but there is only one room and we can't have two girls in it. I have a booking now, so I need you to go out.'

She left, going to the other room, and I slammed the door behind her and started to get ready, not caring what they were talking about. But it was about me, for sure.

10

Wise1safe wanted to meet Kate and asked me to bring her with me to the sauna. It was my first threesome with her, and a chance for us to talk outside of the flat and to get know each other better.

She was nice and friendly. I sensed a change in my feelings for her.

A client wanted an overnight, but Kate was using the room, so I suggested a discount to him and we went to a hotel. I needed to get out of the atmosphere of the flat, as I was feeling suffocated.

I arrived at the hotel, and he was already very stoned. He wanted to be raped and fucked in his arse, asking me to whip him until he bled. I think he was punishing himself. I had been feeling irritated by of all the things that were happening, and I was fed up with these crazy, drugged-out people. He had a sad look. I couldn't understand it at all.

But however I felt about it, bondage, domination and strap-ons had become my most popular services. One of my best clients was scheduled to come in the late afternoon. I arrived early to make sure the room would be available, which was already a very unpleasant situation to be in.

While I was setting up the room, Fernanda was in the other room with

Kate and another supposed friend who planned to stay the night. Soon after I got there, her boy arrived with two other friends.

It was summer and they were going to have a barbecue on the terrace. The boy was probably going to use us girls to entertain his friends.

They were all sitting on the terrace drinking when one of them came up to me, saying, 'Come here, *mamita*. Come have some fun with us.'

I said, 'Thanks, babe, but I am not your *mamita*.' (*Mamita* means 'mummy' in Spanish.)

'Look, I have a booking in a few minutes,' I continued. 'It's gonna be ninety minutes. Please can you all stay out here on the terrace and not go inside the flat. If my client notices that there is a party here, he will feel uncomfortable during his rather unusual session. If anyone needs to go to the bathroom, please go quietly, one by one. I will let you guys know when I'm done.'

They were already sniffing some coke. One of the boys laughed. 'Are you gonna fuck your client's arse or are you gonna whip him?'

'That is not your business,' I replied.

My client arrived. I tied him to the bed and the session started.

At some point, we started hearing noises outside the room, giggling and whispering.

He said, 'There are people outside the door. I thought we were alone here.'

'It must be my colleague with her boyfriend.'

'But they should not be spying on us. I cannot continue the session. I have lost all rhythm. Release me, I want to leave.'

'Let me go out and check what is going on. Can you wait a bit? Please?'

But he was feeling very uncomfortable and insisted on leaving the flat.

I was very upset, as I had just lost my best client.

I went out to the terrace where they were having their party and start to yell at them.

'I asked to you all to stay on the terrace. Just for ninety minutes. The food and drink you are enjoying are here because of this job. You guys are so useless, you come here for free fun, free food and free drinks. You're idiotic and poor of mind and have no money. Useless is what you all are.'

Fernanda interrupted, shouting back at me. 'What are you talking about? This is my house; they are my friends. Do not talk to us like that.'

'Yes, you're right. This is your house. You chose your friends. I'm leaving this place. I thought you were *my* friend.'

When I turned to leave, I heard someone whisper *puta*. (*Puta* means slut in Spanish.)

I turned back, my face burning with rage.

'Well, someone just called me *puta*. Who was it?'

And they all bowed their heads. They were all very stoned.

I asked again: 'Who called me *puta*?'

Again, all were silent.

'I'll say one thing. Yes, I am a slut, but I choose what I want to be and who I want to be a whore for.'

I looked at Fernanda, who was very pale and quiet, sitting with her head down. 'And it seems like you already chose the level of whore you want to be, my friend. I feel sorry for you. Three guys in this room and no one has the balls to tell to my face who called me *puta*.

'So this message will be for all three of you; I will turn around again to leave this fucking place. Call me *puta* again and what I did with my client in that room, I will do to each of you. I will tie you up and fuck the arse of each one of you, calling all three of you my *putas*, and I promise to take my time and not use any kind of lube.' And then I left.

I went down to my Lambretta and burst into tears. I was shaking; fear was mixed with anger and the wish to break anything I could get my hands on. I took a deep breath and rode home in a hurry, watching the mirrors, afraid that someone could be following me. I was desperate to lie down on my bed and rest.

At 3:00 a.m., the phone rang. Kate was in tears.

'Come here, please. One of them locked himself in the bathroom with Fernanda and is abusing her.'

'Where are the others?' I asked.

'They are in the other room completely fucked. They are very drugged up. Fernanda will not stop screaming and crying and nobody is doing anything. Call the police or call your friends, please,' she asked desperately.

'She told me that it is her house and her friends, no? So, though it hurts my heart to say it, I can only tell you that it is her problem. I am not gonna help. You call the police,' I said, hanging up the phone. But I cried all night, feeling helpless and guilty for not doing anything.

I still had the key to the flat, so the next day I went to get my stuff. I dropped a message to Fernanda, asking that no one be there. Only her. Then I called Kate to ask her exactly how the night ended.

'They were taking drugs and made us suck and give them fun. Then, one got hold of Fernanda's hand and they went into the toilet. Suddenly, Fernanda was crying and screaming for help. Nobody did anything, they just ignored her. That's when I called you. When you refused to come, I got a big wooden spoon from the kitchen and started to bang on the door until the guy got very annoyed. He opened the door very angry and I hit him with the spoon so many times. Fernanda went and got a knife, asking all of them to leave. They were so fucked up. They left, but they couldn't even walk properly.'

I arrived at the flat and grabbed my stuff, giving Fernanda the key and telling her, 'I already know what happened here last night. Tell me who it was and I'll make the son of a bitch pay for it. Let's go to the police. I will be with you.'

She looked at me in disbelief. 'What do you think the police will do? Put me in jail as a madam? I do not want that. Don't mess around. Do you want to leave? If so, go and forget this house.'

I reached out to hold her hands. 'I feel so sorry for you, my friend. You do not deserve to end up like this. You are addicted to cocaine and can't think straight anymore. That guy is giving you drugs so you can do more bookings. He is not capable of protecting you. You don't need him. I can protect you.'

'Go!' she said.

I took my things and, as I left, I swore that 'I will never set foot in this flat again.' I had no idea what to do or what was going to happen next. I was so desperately sad.

11

I needed to reorganise my situation, so I spent a few days at home, locked in my room, thinking about what to do, bursting with anger, crying so much, feeling so powerless. How I wished I could punish those useless guys, but I also considered how silly Fernanda was to allow all those things to happen.

I grabbed my phone and started to search for last-minute hotel deals. I found one for three days in Chelsea. It seemed too posh, but I decided to try. I had nothing to lose. It felt like moving from Brooklyn to Manhattan.

Working in central London felt scary to me, a rich area with beautiful façades and glamorous mansions, but I needed to try. I needed a change, as the area where I had been working was too rough.

I'd never been to Chelsea, so I walked into this hotel with my mind completely blank and my hands sweating, feeling so alone.

I missed my friend, as I didn't have anyone to talk to about this. Fernanda was not there to laugh with me anymore. How would it be for me, to work alone? Now was the time to find out: I got a message from the client telling me he had arrived. I gave him my room number.

A very distinguished, well-dressed gentleman was at my room door. Well, for starters, I was not used to seeing men be well-dressed. Peckham was more about wearing jeans under the butt, leaving almost all their underwear on show.

I opened a bottle of wine and offered the client a glass. After the session, we talked a little. I needed to share my frustrations with someone and he seemed so nice. He gave me the tip of not telling a client the number of my room straightaway, but having them first get to the floor. Then I could give them the number, to avoid unwanted extra people.

He had been using the site for a long time. He explained to me how girls work when they are independent. He gave me the confidence to look for a small apartment for myself in London, where I would be able to meet better clients. Obvious things really, but at that moment, this was what I needed to hear from someone like him.

In those three days at the hotel, I had only three new clients. I was glad that I already had some faithful clients who, knowing my situation, came to visit me.

I was feeling lost and needed to rent a flat.

'How's business?' My friend Paolo asked me when he arrived at the bar, greeting me with a kiss on the forehead and ordering a beer. He had been my best friend for a while and I need to get it all it out, so I told him about what happened at Fernanda's house.

He sighed. 'You should have called me. I can always get some guys to scare those sons of bitches,' he replied, squeezing my shoulder. Then he asked, 'What now? Are you going come out of this life or what?'

'No, I need to get an apartment in Central London to start working as an independent and meet new clients. I can't do it at my house where my daughter is, and it needs to be in Central London, but it is too expensive. I don't declare enough income to be able to get one.'

'Find the flat and I can put it in my name. And let me know if you need some money, as I am your brother.'

I started my search and, as a first step, I rented a studio in South Kensington in Paolo's name, but I didn't feel happy about it. What happened at Fernanda's house kept haunting me. I often woke up in the middle of the night having a panic attack. I spoke to Kate again, who told me through tears that the boy hit Fernanda's because she was jealous about him being with another woman. I wasn't surprised to hear that they were still not doing well.

The studio was small and the decor was not good, consisting of only a wardrobe and a metal bed that would surely break during the first fuck. And it was on the fourth floor, without a lift.

But it was listed by the only agency that did not ask me for a huge list of documents. I changed the position of the 'furniture,' but it still was not looking very good. I listed myself as available on my profile, though, as I had no money. I had spent everything on the deposit to rent this flat.

The phone rang, and I got my first booking. I gave him my address, got ready, and then the bell rang. When I opened the door, I saw a pale man, exhausted from the stairs. He was struggling to breathe.

I gave him a glass of water. He looked at me, looked around the flat, and then apologised. 'I am sorry, but I don't want to stay.' And then he left. I closed the door behind him and said, 'Good start' to myself. This was not a suburb where you only needed a bed to open your legs.

The second step was to change the decor. I used my credit card to buy a new bed, rugs, pictures and candles. I needed to make the place nice and cosy.

There's a saying, 'Don't shit where you eat.' I kept this place only to meet my clients and went back every night to my home where I lived with my daughter, who was now almost sixteen years old. This was the same routine I had when I was using Fernanda's flat to work.

My real home, the place where I lived, slept and was a mum, was so messy. But I missed it when I wasn't there during the day and when I couldn't wake up with the noise of my dog running along the corridor to my room, a sign that my daughter was leaving for school.

My dog would jump on my bed, waiting for me to take her to the park. I would drink coffee and read my emails until she became impatient. Then we'd go. She was always happy and desperate, wagging her tail.

That was my routine every morning and she kept me fit, as we would cover about four miles a day; she never had enough of running and playing. Rain or sun, we were out there in the mornings. After that, we'd return home, I'd feed her, cook some lunch and leave it on the stove for my daughter to have when she got back from school. I'd always leave nice notes or messages, even just 'I love you', on the board hanging on the kitchen wall.

Then I'd get on my Lambretta and go to the new place, which I called 'my office'.

On my way, once a week, I stopped off to see this guy who sold flowers on the street in the centre of Kensington. I would clean my office, put my flowers in a vase, make up my face and choose my outfit. Then I'd be ready to attend to my bookings.

Still, my phone was not busy. My profile had only around ten to fifteen views a day and, on many days, there were no bookings. It was starting to worry me. Things had barely begun and I was already discouraged. But I still I couldn't forget what happened at Fernanda's house.

An Indian man in a huge turban came one day, looked me over, and walked away. So, things were not prospering like I'd wished. I was very upset, so I called Jim, my sweet toy boy who came on his trousers. I went to his house, and he made me an amazing Bolognese.

We were doing well. He was taking longer to cum and made me feel good. He was only a young guy, but was already very responsible, mature and humble in his being, and he gave me total inner peace.

He dreamed of being a football coach, but also of getting married and having many children. He loved children and, that night, while I was adoring his face, I told him, 'I could be your mum.'

He smiled and said, gently, 'Luckily, you are not. We are not deceiving each other or making promises. We are only being good to each other.

What's the problem?'

And, in my thoughts, I wished to be younger, to be able to compete for the heart of that boy who was so full of values.

One morning, I went to my manicurist in Elephant and Castle. On the way back to my office, I stopped at a traffic light and spotted Fernanda crossing the street, holding hands with her boyfriend.

Kate told me that he had fled to Spain, as the police were searching for him. She was wearing huge sunglasses to hide her black eye.

Our eyes met. I was in shock, unable to speak or move, but she ran towards to me, stopping the traffic, and said, 'Talk to me.' My only response was, 'This is your life and your problem. I don't need any explanation.'

I arrived at my office very angry. How could I let myself get so down because of all this, when she doesn't even value herself? I couldn't do anything but take care of my own life.

12

The third step was to make my profile more exciting. I needed to get busy.

I sent a message to Lee:

Darling, I am not busy. Can you please help me to make some changes on my profile? Write something exciting? I am desperate. I'm not going to even pay the rent.

Oh, my dear. Look at the place where you chose to go. Kensington is full of young girls and beautiful ones, too, so the competition is hard. You were crazy to have chosen there.

Oh, thank you. You are being very helpful. I ask you for help and you make me feel even worse.

OK, sorry, let me think of some creative things for your profile and I will get back to you.

In the morning, I was almost hysterical when I read his message: *Morning, love, from now you need to log in as CumFuckMyArse.*

I thought I was having an hallucination when I read my profile. It was all about being an anal provider. Both ways. Giving and receiving.

MY ADVERT:

MY USP IS I LOVE IT UP THE ARSE

Hi, I am Lily,

I am nice looking, sexy, fit and a firm-bodied lady. I am very genuine, simple, friendly, with a good sense of humour. I enjoy every single thing on my 'like list'.

I describe myself as an angel raised by the devil. My appetite for adventurous sex is huge and I love to be satisfied, as well as to give you the ultimate satisfaction. I'm self-possessed, sincere, natural and supremely confident and my physical charms are every bit as enticing as my steamy attitude.

Use your imagination and chose the role play:

Imagine me on top riding you, or you bending me over, on my knees, or taking me however you prefer, or a bit more with you fucking me from behind, pulling my hair, or just while I lick her pussy. (Yeahhh, I do like pussy as well.)

Want to get even more kinky? I can use my bondage skills: I've got ropes, collars, bed ties, whips and my vibrators, dildos, ball ring with a vibrating rabbit, and a WE VIBE which we both control, an electro-sex stimulator and many more. (Actually, I am a toy addict.)

A level? Oooh yeah. I really enjoy it, you will see me going crazy as you're fucking my arse while I play with my clit, using my bullet, or I can introduce you to my 5, 6, 7 and 8-inch strap-ons. One of the sets vibrates or, if you are not experienced, we can start with me just playing with my fingers and tongue and then let it go.

Notice, domination and humiliation are different. Domination doesn't necessarily need to humiliate the other person (I DO NOT DO HUMILIATION). I spank, I use naughty and dirty talk, but I don't use offensive language.

Would you like to bend over to my feet?? They are very cute and small and always painted with nicely coloured varnish, ready to be kissed. Ready?

On your arrival, I will offer you a drink from my good selection of cognac, whisky, spirits and wine. (I have good taste as I enjoy drinking.) We have five minutes to toast and break the ice before we start to play. I am not a clock watcher. I want you to feel comfortable, satisfied and to come back to visit me again.

MY TOYS

- 8 SIZES OF STRAP-ON

- VIBRATORS

- BUTT PLUGS

- SPECULUM

- NIPPLE CLIPS

- ELECTRO STIMULATION (with a cock ring, prostate plug stimulator, Electra pads)

-2 SIZES OF PROSTATE VIBRATOR MASSAGER

- COCK RING WITH BALL STRAP

- VIBRATING COCK RING WITH A CLIT RABBIT

- BED STRINGS, COLLARS, ROPES, WHIPS, ETC ...

- AND YOUR FINGERS TO PLAY WITH ME

'What do you think?' he asked me.

'What? You must be crazy! Don't you think it is a little exaggerated? Vulgar? I need to compete with beautiful young ladies and you just write something filthy? Is this a joke?'

Then he called me straightaway, saying: 'Firstly, this is you! Put yourself in the place of the clients: they go on a website, they want to screw and they are horny. It is a big catalogue, with so many offers. You are there and need to be picked. The pages are full of photos with beautiful and amazing girls.

'Too many choices confuses the client. Those who are interested in something that is referred to as young, a princess, a model, a body to die for or the best are not for you. Hook your own kind of client.'

'Act as bait. Even if they don't enjoy your services, they won't be able to resist clicking to read your profile. With more views, you will go to the top of the page. And then, you will hook your client. Sell what you like, not what you can't offer. Remember, it is a fuck website, not for dating. Don't be shy or an angel when men are horny. Let's make this a trial run. If, in one week, things do not improve, then you can change your profile again.'

I agreed and, after a week, he texted me asking how things were and if I want to change it again. I just replied, 'No, thanks. I love my new profile.'

The graph showing the people who visited my page was impressively up. From five to ten views in a day, I started to have seventy to a hundred. Not bad! And my phone finally started to ring, too.

But, of course, I attracted all kinds of men – time-wasters and lots of nasty people, unfortunately. It was good to learn how to deal with them, though, and I think I learnt a big lesson in Peckham, so I could handle it.

I would classify clients into three types.

The Collector: the man who loves being with different types of women just to collect numbers. This type of client rarely comes back. They only need to tick a box. They need to always be with different, more beautiful and better women.

The Sex-Deprived: married or single guys who have no time for or interest in dating. They look for a girl in order to escape or relieve their stress. Some want a regular escort to whom they can come and get what they need, but often they will see different girls.

The Kinky: the ones who share the same sexual tastes as me. I choose those who like bondage, anal sex and strap-ons. This type of man never goes to different women because the most essential thing was their confidence and well-being during the meeting. Usually, they are faithful and will always be there for me because they need to feel comfortable. Yes, they are the ones I want.

I gave my studio a very nice atmosphere, with a minibar and a good selection of fine spirits. The fridge was stocked with wines and prosecco. I even bought more toys and posted pictures with them. I became a dominant anal player lover.

Every client, when he arrived, was offered a drink. It became a ritual and they seemed to love it. I wanted my place and my presence to make my clients feel like they were in a shelter where they could feel relaxed and safe. That's how I would get them to come back.

I did have one rather quirky client during that time. He wanted to be strangled by my legs. He struggled, so I needed to be stronger to have him locked in the middle of my legs. The more he fought in vain, the more he became excited and masturbated. At the end of the session, he told me, 'I'll come back and keep coming back again until the day that I can be stronger than your legs. Then I won't see you again.'

I was glad I did ju-jitsu for long time when I was young, as that was what made me good at holding the client. But, one day, he won and he never came to see me again.

My new profile views continued to go up. Feedback was welcome and very helpful. I started to get more bookings and saw a difference in the clients. I wasn't even thinking about Peckham and Fernanda anymore. But that doesn't mean I totally forgot about it.

From a handsome Frenchman to a Scandinavian guy with a huge dick, people of different countries and ethnicities turned up, including a client who wanted to play with being tied up and teased with ice. My bookings were getting more diverse, interesting and fun, longer and unhurried. I stopped needing to look at my watch.

I was having new sexual experiences and pushing my boundaries and, honestly, my sex drive was getting higher. I dressed as a housekeeper for Nit, who wanted a full service. My English was improving very fast and I was no longer struggling to the end of the month.

13

I got an email from someone who made the biggest offer I had ever accepted:

Good morning:

I am a businessman, well paid, English, white, born and bred, middle-aged and a lover of BDSM. I saw your profile and found it very interesting. I believe you may be the person I'm looking for.

I'm offering you £2,500 to have a BDSM session in a dungeon for five hours.

It will include whipping your back, and then you will be tied up and hung, so I can fuck you. If you agree, I will call you today at the time of your choice and we will discuss the date, time and any questions. To give you the security that I am not a waste of time, a deposit will be made.

Looking forward to hearing from you

Regards

L

Getting £2,500 for five hours? Of course, I want to discuss it!

Hi Mr L, Yes. I would love to discuss this meeting please.

He phoned me the same day and we had a chat. His voice was calm and strong. He was a very polite Englishman. We agreed the terms of the meeting and what I would and wouldn't accept. After the call, he sent me another email with his like list of services, and I had to agree in writing. A £500 deposit was made on the same day into my bank account.

I came to his dungeon, he let me in and we had some drinks. I needed some alcohol. I was used to BDSM and the dungeon really excited me, but this would be my first time getting hung without having my feet or back propped up on the floor or on a bed. We were not alone though. There was another man and that made me nervous. I started having scary thoughts.

'Who is he?' I asked. Mr L said, 'He is the person who will tie you up. He is a professional, a *shibari* expert. Have some drinks to relax.'

BDSM is inspired by *shibari*, an ancient Japanese cult of ropes, used by samurai to restrain captives and during torture, but also to transport prisoners to their villages, where many times they decapitated them to demonstrate their power after they had defeated the enemy.

As agreed, I took twenty lashes, more than enough to mark my back. I was tied on a St Andrew's cross and whipped by the *shibari* expert, while Mr L was there just enjoying the scenario. Mr L approached me then, with a hard cock.

'You are a good girl; I want you as my slave as you have a strong back.'

Then he began to nuzzle my neck, rubbing his body against me and touching me everywhere. He was a very attractive man, wearing good perfume, and the pain in my back was nothing.

I was still shitting myself though. 'This is a real game,' I thought.

He released me and I fought with myself to not show how insecure I was. We had more drinks and were already having body contact. He was sitting on the sofa and I sat on top of him in the cowgirl position, but with no penetration. We were rubbing against each other for almost an hour. Now it was time for the hardest part of the session. The *shibari* expert came in and tied me in those beautiful knots, enveloping my body and leaving me hanging with my legs open. Then Mr L came to fuck me, in all holes, with me hanging there, completely immobilised.

This was a dangerous game, as the person must do it properly. I am happy I had the experience, but I will never repeat it. My body was in so much pain from being tied up. I couldn't feel it at the time, but my back had sustained some injuries from the ropes. It is a bad idea to get into situations like this if you don't know what you are doing. In a real game, it is not like the *50 Shades of Grey* movie, and can result in serious consequences.

I had to take a week off due the injuries on my back, so I used the money to go shopping with my daughter. I spent £700; it was the first time I could afford that kind of luxury. I also spent £800 on an old VW. I needed a spare key, so a guy came to my house to make it.

'How long have you lived here?' he asked me.

'Six years, but I am thinking of moving house,' I said.

He asked me, sarcastically, 'Where do you want to go? Kensington?'

Laughing, I replied: 'I wish I could afford it.'

I felt welcome in Central London and it was a very positive time. All the nice people I met lifted my self-esteem. A few months back, I had been without a job, frustrated, a shy mother who never had a strong personality and whose sexual life had been very limited.

But it was not all good. I also had a lot of time-wasters and weird guys who were so annoying.

One night, I had three bookings let me down, but, at 10:00 p.m., I had an outcall request to Mayfair.

I went to a luxurious Victorian hotel. My legs were shook as I entered this glamorous building I would never have imagined one day visiting as a guest. The doorman helped me inside, and I hoped the receptionist wouldn't stop me to ask for the room number. I had parked my car away from the building, and then changed into heels, but I barely knew how to walk in them. I never went out in heels. My foot size is two and a half and it is impossible to find high heels in London in that size.

I felt like I was inside a castle and I was terrified of entering the room, afraid that the client would not like me because I was far from being tall and sophisticated.

Neil was a lovely businessman though, who seemed to have a lot of money. He looked at me and said, 'Great. Exactly how I like it. Beautiful and simple.'

'Do you mind if I take my shoes off?' I asked him.

He said, gently, 'Oh, please, make yourself comfortable. I'd prefer you naked anyway.' We both laughed.

It had been about ten months since I started this new life. My daughter would call me every day to find out where I was. When I wasn't around, if she needed anything, she called my friend Paulo or my sister, who tracked me from her phone when I was visiting clients. If I were alone, this life would have been easier and I could have made more money. But my daughter was priceless. Having a home and going to my office was also quite exciting. I felt I was living two different lives, and I needed both. But I was also messing my daughter about and it was not fun, so I decided to tell her the truth. She was almost 18 years old, old enough, and we always had a very close and open relationship. I am more than a parent for her; we are like best friends. I just needed to find the right words to say.

I took her to eat at a restaurant of her choice. She loves Italian food.

I jumped in. 'I have another apartment and sometimes I sleep there because I use it to meet friends and that is why there are many days when I don't come home.'

'Why do you have to pay rent for an apartment to meet guys?'

'I have some friends who help me financially, so I use the flat to see them.'

'Mum, are you an escort?'

I choked and couldn't breathe. I felt like my legs might collapse. I was pale, but I said, as calmly as I could, 'Kind of.'

'Well, you're single and I see that you're happier and less stressed. I suspected that was what you were doing as I don't see any more overdue bills and the fridge is always full of things of better quality. And you never said where you worked. The only thing that made me upset was knowing that you were hiding something from me, that you had a secret and did not trust me. Also, I get so worried when you don't come home. Now I know where you sleep. Do what you think you must if it makes you happy. Just please, don't find a boyfriend if you need to lie to him, and please, keep it secret from others, as I need that.'

My daughter, once again, impressed me with her maturity. I felt as if I had taken a load off my shoulders. I was totally relieved. I was not sure if telling her was the right or wrong choice, but she behaved with such understanding and made me feel so much better. I was still not sure of her feelings about my new life, though. I needed to see how she would deal with it.

14

Mr Handsome booked me again at the same hotel, the St. Pancras Renaissance, where I met him the first time with Mrs Kinky and the Fireman. 'Please don't forget the seamed stockings.'

I went shopping in the afternoon. My business had been improving slowly but steadily. I was meeting much better clients and visiting nice hotels, which is much safer than going to clients' houses.

I arrived at the hotel more relaxed than last time. I walked straight to the bar, and there they were.

Mrs Kinky was so elegant and friendly, a person able to entertain anyone, just having fun. She made me feel comfortable and we laughed all night. Mr Handsome was very polite and wanted me to get tipsy, and the Fireman had an incredible sense of humour. I was so glad to be there again.

'How was your day?' I asked Mrs Kinky, trying to keep up the conversation.

'It was great. I spent all day in a dungeon with my Fireman.'

'She tied me up in the bed and, using a spiky hairbrush, hit me all over my back, including my butt. It is a bit sore,' the Fireman said, touching his butt with a comical expression of pain.

'Lucky you weren't hanging,' I said jokingly, thinking of my recent injuries.

Then I asked him, 'Do you enjoy that? Because I do like whips, but not that hard. Is that why you are standing? Are you bleeding?'

'Oh, fuck yeah I do. But I do have my limits and she already knows that. My butt is very sore.'

He looked at her and she smiled charmingly. 'This is why I cannot say no to her, she is stunning.'

'How did you find him?' I asked her.

'Oh, Lily. I took a while to find a good one.' She smiled, looking at him. Mr Handsome was laughing, as they sat holding hands.

'How can they have so open a relationship?' I wondered to myself, but he seemed to be reading my mind.

'I don't do jealousy, Lily, if is that is what you're thinking. We have had thirty years of happy marriage.'

After having enjoyed the bar, we went straight to the room, my tasks had to be done.

'There's a house in Harlow that they rent by the day, and it has two bedrooms. I want to go on Friday and come back on Sunday. Do you want to come?' Kate asked me.

'Things are quiet, so, yes, let's go change it up a bit.'

She spent the night before at my flat and we left for Harlow on Friday; I drove. It was a decent house and we spent all day doing nothing. I got so many messages, but no one showed up.

In the afternoon, I said to Kate, 'I am so frustrated, I'm going back to London.' But that's when I got another message.

Hi Lily, I am hoping you are available tonight, two-hour outcall for some BDSM fun.

Well, I wasn't busy at all, but I also suspected this was another time-waster.

Hi there. Yes, I am free, but didn't bring any rope or collars with me.

That's OK. I have enough stuff here, hope you brought your toy box and, yes, A level will probably happen.

I will bring my toys.

My address is at a garage. I have a flat above it, but it's much more fun playing with the ramps. I will send you a booking request so you can feel safe and see my feedback.

I started freaking out.

Great, I can come any time you tell me, but not too late as I need to drive back to London. Are you interested in two girls, by any chance? My friend is very interested in seeing us playing on a ramp.

(Bullshit. I am freaking out and I don't want to go to a garage alone.)

How much?

Make us an offer and please be generous. (I was up to take any offer, though, rather than going alone.)

Kate and I were looking at each other with our fingers crossed. He made an offer.

Hmm. OK. Deal.

Great. See you both at 6.30.

I dressed in my PVC outfit and put on my boots, and we both went to the meeting. The GPS took me to a street that was very secluded and poorly lit. We saw a huge hangar. It was already dark and it felt like a horror movie. The perfect scenario for a serial killer. We looked at each other, questioning whether to go inside. But we walked in, and the performance had to start.

When an escort meets a client, they need to leave any fear or shyness behind. You are what you sell; so, you put on a face and never show weakness, in order to gain their respect. It doesn't matter if your legs are shaking or your heart is jumping through your throat.

He came to greet us, saying he wanted to play on the ramp. I took off my long coat and gave it to him to hang up. Under it, I was wearing only my little PVC top, a G-string and long knee-high boots with killer heels.

'Wow, very nice,' he said.

He walked inside and we followed him until we got to the car ramp. He picked up some zip ties and he tied me up with my arms stretched out. I felt like Jesus on the cross. Then he ordered Kate to wear the strap-on. He takes my whip and gives it to Kate, saying, 'I do not hit women, but you will.'

I can't see them because I have my back turned, but, knowing her, I was sure she was shaking with fear. In fact, her first hits aren't firm and the whip does not strike hard enough, so I say, 'Stronger.' She started to hit harder.

Already tired, I got down on my knees, still with my hands tied like on the cross, and looked over at the client. He read my mind and lowered his pants while I sucked him. Kate came from behind me with the strap-on and then, after, it was his turn. I couldn't see anything, but I felt his cock getting bigger and harder and, clearly, he was ready to cum, when Kate screamed, 'Oh my God, he is falling down! Lily, he is not well, what do I do?'

I shouted, 'Set me free, quickly. Cut off the zip ties!'

She was clumsy as she panicked. 'How?'

And then he got a Stanley knife from somewhere nearby and gave it to her to cut the ties before he fell on the floor. We took him to the kitchen to drink water and, after he calmed down, he told us he was fine. But he must have had some health problems he didn't want to tell us about.

Back in the car, I looked at Kate and we both took a deep breath. I said, 'I think we've had enough adventure for today. Let's go home.'

On the way back to London, I got a message from Neil, that customer from the posh hotel in Mayfair.

I am in London, out with some clients. Just finished an important business fair and had lots of drinks. Come join me ...

'Oh, how embarrassing. How am I going to pick him up in my horrible old car? I am not even dressed properly to meet him,' I said to Kate. But I went. In one hour, I arrived in Soho and he came out of the restaurant.

'Let's get out of here, I've had too much to drink.'

I drove to his hotel and he was indeed very drunk. It was another beautiful place in Russell Square. I laid him on the bed, as he was in a very bad way. We had a short chat and I left. What he needed was a good sleep.

The day after, I texted the guy from the garage:

I just want to thank you for yesterday. It was a great experience, but I left a bit worried about you.

Yes. I am good. Just too much excitement for one night. Hope you two had as much fun as I did.

Oh, yes. We did and laughed all night. Kate was happy to have fucked me. She had never done anything like that before.

That week, the only 'normal man' who I met was a lovely and friendly Korean lawyer. He left work very late and wanted to have some sex to relieve his stress.

15

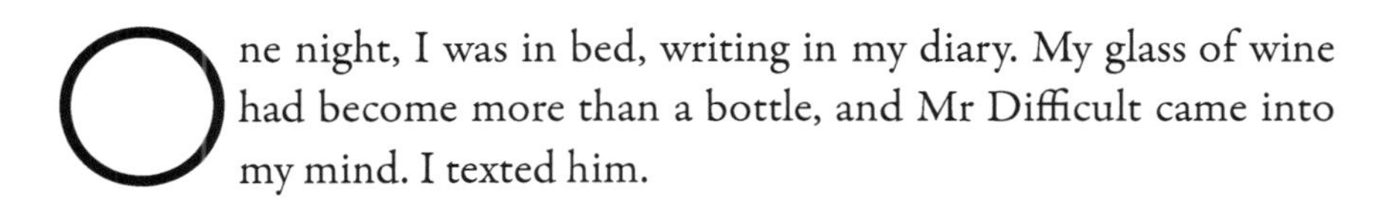

One night, I was in bed, writing in my diary. My glass of wine had become more than a bottle, and Mr Difficult came into my mind. I texted him.

If the Mountain will not come to Muhammad, then Muhammad must go to the mountain. How are you?

I'm fine, in Japan. Trying to eat my lunch but this is a little tasteless and undercooked.

And he sent a photo of *sukiyaki*, a plate with many vegetables, which you must cook at your table.

You should cook it and try a little shoyu and spice.

He replied ten minutes later: *Yes. Tastes better.*

I still think of you very often. Why do you think I fell for you?

Perhaps because you know you cannot have something and it makes you want it even more.

Perhaps you are right. And what makes a man desire two girls together as you do? When the most of time, the girls don't even get satisfied?

Selfishness, power, dominance. I had this feeling about you.

I closed my eyes and fell asleep.

'My husband has a meeting this week. Our sex life is a disaster. I think he doesn't love me anymore. I would like to try an experience with a woman.'

'I know how hard the frustration is when you're not being desired by your husband. Come to see me and we can have some naughty time together. Sometimes, it is just about getting out of our routine, and a little adventure raises our self-esteem.'

She was a mother of three kids, a woman who didn't work and dedicated her life to her family. She was very nervous, so I needed to break the ice and make her relax, or it was not going work. I was anxious, too.

It was her first time doing this and it was my first time having a lady as a client on my own. But I didn't want to ask her too many questions, as she seemed quiet and lacking self-esteem, and was already agitated enough.

'White wine or prosecco?' I asked her and she said, 'Prosecco sounds good.'

I sat on the sofa beside her, but not too close, and poured some prosecco. Even then, I could feel the beating of her heart as we started to chat.

'I still have fantasies, but I feel that I am not allowed to do anything different. I visit adult content websites and I feel so turned on, but when I am with my husband, I just can't ask him to do anything different. I feel so blocked. It is so boring and he is not even interested. I always wanted to try a threesome or a girl, but I am so scared of his judgment. I don't want him to think that I am lesbian, because I am not. I just haven't had many experiences, and now, I feel that the time is passing and I am missing out.'

I listened to her, as she needed to talk.

'On my side, as a working girl, my clients are mostly married. My services are all about anal and all kinds of different services, except the vanilla ones. So many guys enjoy prostate massages, strap-ons, cross-dressing and so on. I never thought of anyone who I met for that sort of service as being gay, but also, they feel embarrassed about asking for or sharing this enjoyment with their wives. And so many have been with cross-dressers and transgender people and they are also straight. People's minds are unlimited. Adventures and trying new things spice up a relationship, but the fear of judgment in our society ruins opportunities to free ourselves from these taboos. But this doesn't make anyone a bad parent or partner or even a bad human being.'

She was now clearly feeling more relaxed, so I approached and I kissed her. She responded and I undressed her, going down on her. She was wet, but she did not come. I wanted to believe that I did a good thing with her and we ended the afternoon a bit tipsy, laughing and gossiping about life, men, husbands and the system.

Al was one of my regulars and a cross-dresser for over five years. He already had his own big box with his collection of silk panties that he kept in my room. I always wore silk panties, stockings or hold ups to match his.

He had a great job and was happily married. He always brought good wine and ensured a great evening. He admitted, 'I am a nymphomaniac, I have to masturbate three times a day.'

What makes me feel good about this kind of booking, honestly, I don't know. It was just a good sensation to be transgressive and, with some clients, when I dress as a man, I take control and I fantasise they are my whore.

Others are very normal, but just enjoy wearing women's clothes. I know a musician who enjoys the texture of stockings so much that even his underwear is made with this fabric.

Being what you're not, or being weak and submissive when you are a powerful person in real life, is maybe the key to this desire, but I don't know. What I know is that all my bitches and cross-dressers are normal people, and many are rich and powerful with very important jobs – and they make me feel powerful, being what I am not with them, too.

I named Ashy, my other cross-dresser, as 'my bitch'.

He was a very rich businessman from Egypt. He told me how his adolescence had been.

Imagine, fifty years ago, being in a Muslim country as a young fourteen-year-old, with hormones flowing and the smell of pussy passing only in a dream. Hands can be used, but it becomes boring. Still, it was the only option for those poor, horny boys.

One day, he met a guy who was older, with a big one, who 'abused' him. The word 'abused' being used here because he was only fourteen, but he did consent. Still, this is unacceptable to many. But I am not here to judge.

He told me that this guy 'abused' him for several years. At the beginning, obviously this was a bit confusing for a young guy, but once he got used to it, he loved it. He didn't want it to stop, but he was sent to university and got married. He never saw this man again, but he kept thinking of him.

'Ash, did it affect your life at any point?' I asked him.

He was sipping a single malt, but his answer was clear and firm. 'Oh, no, definitely not. I have a wonderful wife, children, a happy life, but sometimes I miss him. Stereotypical family life is boring after many years. It is my little secret and I enjoy that, because when I think of him, I have fantasies. I would pay any money to see this man again. I want you to dress me with the lingerie I bought, make me up and call me "bitch". Use your bigger strap-on and I will close my eyes and see him.'

So, I did what he wanted. 'You look lovely,' I said to him.

He showed off in front of me, holding the glass of whisky. I put him in a doggie-style position and spanked his bottom and then I took my red lipstick, wrote 'my bitch' on his butt and took a picture, as we both laughed.

In fact, every time he lands in London, he texts me:

Your bitch has arrived.

I'd now met Mr Handsome a few times, and I was going again to the St. Pancras Renaissance. I had only just found out that the number listed on the bookings was not from his phone. He had never texted me or arranged our meetings. It was all from the Fireman.

'Who is this man?' I asked myself, feeling a bit uncomfortable about not knowing who I was texting. Then he said, 'Come on, Lily, you surely have two different numbers and never give us your private one.'

I replied with a smile. 'Yes, you are right.'

He said, 'OK, let's to do a deal. I will give you my number. I only have one. Are you gonna give me your personal one?'

'Sure,' I said. He gave me his phone and I typed in my number. He told me, 'From today, I will be the one to text you; and now, will you please go to the toilet. I want to observe your beautiful legs.'

How he loved to see me arrive at the bar of the hotel, or walk anywhere. It didn't matter what else I was wearing, he just loved my legs in seamed stockings. It was incredible how he would stare at my legs and get turned on.

A stocking fetish is one the most common ones; so many men have it. Mr Handsome has a reason for his fetish. When he was a teenager, he used to watch his auntie walking to work, always wearing seamed stockings, and she was so beautiful that he would go to his bedroom to wank, thinking of her legs. Naughty teenage things.

16

I had an outcall booking at a gay escort's house and I had to meet his sugar daddy. The request was for me and the young guy to tie him up and do some domination. It was exciting to join them for my first time, with two guys having intercourse. It was also my first time seeing someone smoking crack, and it made me a bit uncomfortable. We did BDSM on this erotic hammock fitted in the bedroom. The boy and I didn't use anything, but the customer was completely stoned. I left the flat thinking that was another experience to add to my collection.

One day, Peter, a Swiss guy, knocked on my door. He was very tall, very bald and very polite – just my type.

I opened the door, and straightaway I grabbed his balls. He'd brought a bottle of wine and, while I was preparing the ice bucket, he jumped in the shower.

He came out from the shower with a towel wrapped around his waist. I pulled it aside to check what was there and smiled with satisfaction at what I found. I poured some wine and we toasted each other. I was amazed by how many nice people I was meeting. It was a very new experience.

We had a connection from the first contact that day. Two days later, he texted me saying that he had spare time and wanted to see me again. I think he liked the fact that he left me complete exhausted; he called me again the week after. Three times in two weeks – how flattered he made me feel.

I was getting very popular. My feedback page had grown and I was able to choose who to meet by talking with them on the phone. I would request a chat before I accepted someone, choosing by their voice. It made me more comfortable about accepting the booking.

Mr Handsome wanted to impress me.

'Are you around the afternoon and night on the 21st of February?'

'Yes. Of course.'

'Good girl. I think you should be a very naughty lady, so I can spoil you.'

'What do you have in mind?' I asked.

'The Grove Hotel, Hertfordshire. Now you know my name, and I need to know yours as you will be in the booking. We will be there around 1:00 p.m. Make sure you abuse the spa. Book all your treatments to the room. Whatever you like. I look forward to enjoying you.'

'Wow! That sounds amazing.'

I went online to explore the spa and the venue. I couldn't believe I would be sleeping in that place. It seemed like a castle.

There was a long, narrow road that led to the front of a beautiful building. As I approached, I admired the well-tended, luxurious golf course, watching from afar as some people rode buggies and others played.

They had arrived, in their Range Rover, about thirty minutes before me. I was very embarrassed to be pulling up in my very old VW with the doors falling off. Mrs Kinky saw me arrive and waved from where she sat, smoking a cigar on the terrace of the tearoom. We had tea before exploring the hotel. As we returned to the terrace, she looked at me and smiled, saying, 'Lily, I think you should upgrade your car.'

I said, 'I definitely need to.' We laughed and then the Fireman, who was also smoking a cigar, beckoned and made all of us laugh, before we headed up to the bedroom.

It was almost summertime, so the temperature was just perfect for having dinner later and a few drinks on the cosy terrace where we could enjoy the scent of the countryside. The place was so big and very luxurious. In the morning, I stood in front of the window, contemplating the view of the impeccable golf course.

Mr Handsome came up behind me and said into my ear, 'Look at those people playing golf. You don't know who they are, then?'

'Who are they?'

Mr Handsome removed my bathrobe. 'I am going to fuck you now, right here, and you will be watching this beautiful view from the window and, there, outside playing golf, is the President of the U.S.A. playing with the Prime Minister. Isn't that sight so beautiful?'

My face got pale; my throat was dry. Was I dreaming or what? After that, I had a call telling me it was time to go to my treatment.

The spa was another dream that I didn't want to wake up from. Champagne was served inside the relaxing waiting room. I couldn't believe that a man like him, who has everything, was doing this to impress me.

They like this life and he chose me to enjoy it with them. It was very satisfying, but I needed to learn posher manners. I had a great weekend, feeling that life had been very generous to me as I was enjoying all these things so much.

I got a message from a guy who claimed to be a virgin and wanted to have his first experience with me.

I said to him, 'Look, virgins and young guys are not my thing,' thinking he was going to give up. But then he texted me back:

Lily, I know it might to look silly to you and I know you are so much older than me, but I am really needing a worker as I find it embarrassing going with someone of my age. Please don't think I am a waste of time or some pathetic young boy, I am really interested in meeting. I just want to get rid of my virginity.

So, I thought for ten minutes before I accepted the booking. We agreed on three hours and I asked him to bring his ID card. He was twenty-two and it was fine.

He was a lovely, young, shy guy, and he was clearly nervous. As is my ritual, we had a bottle of bubbles and a little chat and, when I felt he was more comfortable, we started the session.

We met few more times after that, but a virgin doesn't turn me on. Many young guys just need to feel more secure with themselves. It's hard when they are shy and go out and feel incapable of flirting with a girl.

'Hi, are you available tonight for an outcall in Knightsbridge for four hours?'

'Yes, I am. Send me your address.'

'You look great in suspenders.'

I checked the house on Google – he must be a multimillionaire, as it was just beside Harrods, four minutes from my flat.

I rang the bell and the doors opened automatically, so I went inside this big house and felt lost. No one was there to receive me.

A man shouted down, 'Take the stairs and come to the third floor.' I walked through the entrance hall of an impeccably clean house, decorated with antique furniture of high quality, and began climbing the stairs.

I got to the third floor to find the man waiting behind a huge bar. He asked me, 'What do you want to drink?' while placing the envelope on the bar.

'What do you have?' I asked.

'Anything you want.' In fact, the bar had absolutely every kind of drink.

He served me a gin and tonic, then offered me a cigarette, which I accepted. I put the cigarette in my mouth and he lit it. He stared at me, saying, 'You are naughty and I love your profile.'

I noticed his laptop beside him, open to my private gallery. Then, I saw a plate beside him with a mountain of cocaine.

'It's good stuff, have some,' he told me, and I did a big line, hoping not to regret it.

I got high and we start to chat and drink. He was turned on by transgender people, anal sex and pregnant women, so he had a pervy mind. The time was getting on, so I tried to touch him, but he wouldn't let me do it. I didn't understand why until I saw his penis size. It was small. Very small. Already very tipsy and high, we decided to call a few transgender sex workers, but there was no reply, as it was already very late. Then he told me that he knows a big black cock who he wants to watch fucking my ass. He calls him.

Mr Black is an escort who has a huge one.

After introducing ourselves, I told him my nickname on the site, CumFuckMyArse, which made him smile. I asked him:

'What do you sell apart from obviously this very irresistible giant snake between your legs?'

His answer made me spit out my gin and tonic: 'I can make any woman squirt.'

I had to laugh, which seemed to annoy him.

'Are you OK? What is so funny? You don't believe me?'

It's going to be a very interesting night, I thought.

I composed myself and answered, 'Oh, sorry, don't get me wrong, I just remembered something that happened to me a few months ago.'

I told him about Dr Ray and my squirting experience. But I hadn't managed to squirt again since then. So, he said, 'Let's give our client a big show. You will deliver your service, as not many women can take my "snake", but I suppose you can manage, by your advert. And then, I will make you squirt.'

At that point, we were all very high. And I gushed. This time, it was a massive one.

I couldn't believe it. We looked over at the client and his mouth was agape as he masturbated.

I was already out of control and I wanted to play with the client as he was there masturbating, so friendly and gentlemanly, so I touched his butt. I don't really remember much else, but I don't think the night had a happy ending, because he asked me to leave his house.

Mr Black texted me the next morning:

I am worried about you. Did you get home safe?

I can't sleep. I am a bit paranoid.

I will keep talking with you. Drink plenty of water.

Then the messages stopped. Later that afternoon, I was still awake and very down, as that is the reaction I get when I use coke. I was trying to rest, but I spent all day in the dark of my room, crying and very depressed. I found a full box of tablets for sleep in my medical box, so I swallowed few pills and, after thirty minutes without any result, in desperation for sleep, feeling so down and thinking how bad a mother I was and what a bad example I was for my daughter, I took everything which was left in the packet. I only needed sleep and to forget what I had done.

Luckily, my stomach was very upset and I vomited and, after I drank more water, I vomited again. I was feeling very weak and my bloody pressure was very low. I passed out.

I woke up more than twenty-four hours later and I had a text from Mr Black:

Sorry. Yesterday I fell asleep; how are you?

I am terrible. Took so many tablets to sleep that day and got sick and passed out. What happened at the end of the night?

You got very bad. Was a disaster at the end, saying things with no sense. Just out of your mind, but it is OK. The client is used to it.

I went back to sleep. I woke up, after almost two days, very determined: *I won't take drugs anymore.* I had already made that decision and broke it at that house. *And I will not see anyone who does.* And I meant it. That was the last time I used drugs.

But I was interested in Mr Black and his magic fingers.

17

It was an exhausting day; I spent the morning at the gym and my phone had been busy since the day before, with so many different numbers and funny messages. I answered a call, but I couldn't talk as I was working out and people were around, so I accepted the deal this time by message. I left the gym and ran to my flat, which was just around the corner, jumped in the shower and got ready.

I opened the door and saw an arrogant man. He had barely entered when he looked at me from head to foot and said, 'Just from watching you, I don't want to stay.' I stood there, my mind blank, and struggled to answer.

'No problem, just leave,' I managed eventually, pointing to the door. 'I cannot please everyone and I am not a model,' I whispered, consoling myself.

Over time, I have learned to not take it personally. Also, there are so many guys that pay just to feel superior. Some people have the need to degrade a woman to ease their own frustrations. If you don't like me, that is fine, say sorry and leave. But having an arrogant attitude is just poor manners.

A client came to see me and, during the meeting, he told me that I had become very popular in a punter's forum. It is a website where punters write reviews about the girls, and anyone can go in the chat and makes comments and questions, apparently to help others choose a girl to book. A gossip site. I didn't have any idea about the existence of this site, but apparently I was a highlight there, especially because I became a squirter after my meeting with Mr Black.

Women are famous for gossiping, but, trust me, those men, when they talk, particularly on that kind of blog, freely and anonymously behind a screen, and without being verified, they don't have any boundaries and are merciless about women. And they are good at exaggerating.

They write reviews, expecting comments to boost their self-esteem. It's like when boys go to school and they desperately want to fuck the popular girls, but the main pleasure is on the day after when the entire school gets to hear about it.

I was the new victim of their malicious comments and the trophy for those who managed to book me, then write about it. It was just them showing off. In the first posts I read, even those from people who had never met me, they were talking as if they knew me. They made it sound like the girls belonged to the website, and the members were allowed to keep on with their chit-chat, without our permission.

There were a lot of rude comments and questions asking if I was a ladyboy, or if I might be a gender changer, or if I was a porn movie maker, as well as about my age, legal situation and lots of other absurd stuff.

It was quite funny, but also a bit annoying, as it was not only punters reading those posts. There were also bad gangs and pimps masked as clients, using the punters to try to find out about our citizenship status and more, such as if we working girls were alone, where we lived and if we had a pimp or anyone to do security, or CCTV, and so on.

Many girls are not allowed to work or remain in this country. If they don't have a work permit, obviously, they cannot have national insurance and, without it, they cannot have a bank account. Of course, they would never call the police, so those criminals expect to be able to do whatever they want.

Girls on this website can become an easy target for these thugs, who arrive expecting to find sex and some money under the mattress. Also, pimps pretend to be punters in the forum to talk up girls who work for them to try to get them attention. Luckily, they made a mistake about my visa status. But that week I was at the top of that forum and getting many strange calls.

I opened the door and there was this guy with a scary face. He came in and I said, 'Hey, nice to meet you. It is one hour, right? Can we do the paperwork?'

He looked at me very maliciously. 'Hey, babe, relax, I will pay you by pleasing you. You want cocks, I will give you mine.'

Pay me by pleasing me. He was trouble.

I said to him, 'Look, I want to avoid trouble. Can you please leave?'

He was now holding my arm. 'I won't give you any trouble.'

'Take your hands off me. I am calling the police.'

He kept hold of me. 'You're not gonna call the police. You are a whore, so you will let me fuck you.'

My body shuddered and I felt frozen. I was so scared. I tried raising my voice. 'Take your hands off me and go. I will call the police.' And I pushed him.

He persisted. 'Baby, I only want to fuck you, then I will go.' I started to freak out.

'No, get the fuck out of here!' I shouted. 'I will call the police.'

My neighbour started to knock on the wall. She had heard us. He released my arm, so I pushed him out of my place and shut the door.

But he kept knocking on the door! 'Come on, baby, let me fuck you.' I kept quiet behind the door. He left after a few minutes.

I thought about calling the police, but obviously I didn't know if I would get in trouble, as what I was doing was not exactly legal. What if I got a warning or a record? I thought it was better just to leave it and be more careful next time, but it's annoying that we don't feel safe enough to call the police when we need them. I just wanted to cry, but I felt that I needed to find out more about the law in this country.

My neighbour was a Polish lady with three kids. We had met many times in the corridor and I used to play a bit with her kids, especially the littlest one, who was just under a year old.

She had already realised what was going on in my flat, but I didn't see anyone after 10:00 p.m. and I was always very quiet, apart the moans when I was with a client. Her baby cried a lot and I could hear everything, so I supposed she could as well.

She knocked at my door, asking if I was OK. 'If you have any problems, knock the wall hard a few times, and I will call the police. I am sure my kids are annoying when they cry at night, but you never complain. We have been neighbours for over six months now and this is the first time you have had an issue. You are not a problem for us.' I let out a deep breath when she told me that. We smiled at each other and I said, 'Thanks.'

I was so stressed but, luckily, Peter the Swiss guy arrived to see me, so I had a nice client to spend the afternoon with. I didn't want to be alone. He called me every time he landed in London and always arrived with a nice bottle of wine. He made very intelligent conversation, which made me forget about what occurred. But I also needed few big glasses of Chablis.

Mike was a businessman who worked with investors. Tall, very polite, smart-looking and apparently very normal. He talked very calmly; he was the kind of man who gave me a nice and peaceful feeling. He didn't want anything abnormal as a service, so he was another client who I trusted and we became very close. The day after that guy wouldn't leave, we spent the afternoon together.

I told him about the scary guy and he talked to me a bit about the law. It was so nice to have a good client who made me feel safe.

He had an account on that website, and he confirmed that it was really easy to set up a profile as a punter, no one was verified and there was no moderator or rules about what people could post. It also had a private chat, which made it easier to share information. Basically, there was nothing to protect the girls, and no concerns about security. They just wanted people to talk and to get more members and more views, treating the girls like goods to be sold.

I got even angrier when I got a message:

Can you give me a discount and, in exchange, I will write a good review for you.

I made the mistake of answering. *I am afraid that my price is not negotiable.*

In that case, I will write a negative one.

Good luck with that. You should go to work, instead of intimidating me.

How annoyed I felt! I decided to contact the administrator of the website to tell him that it wasn't my choice to be listed and he did not have my consent, so please could he delete all my reviews, as I didn't feel safe. He just ignored me, which solidified my dislike for the website.

AdultWork is the only website where I have my advert. I am free and I have all the control about what is in my profile, including the feedback, as it is my choice whether I want it to appear or not.

Luckily, while all this was going on, I was still having my regular meet-ups with Mr Handsome and Mrs Kinky, my happy millionaire couple. I'd gotten to know them over the last six months of meeting up every two weeks, and enjoyed visits to some of the best hotels in London.

He was a wise and astute businessman, charming in middle age. Thanks to them, I learned good manners and improved my wardrobe.

They just wanted to enjoy life, to escape the stress of being important and any sense of being a 'stereotypical' couple.

One night, we were all going to have dinner and enjoy the beauty of London from the top of The Shard. I met them at the bar on the 52nd floor. This place was stunning, offering a beautiful postcard view of London. Sometimes I still think that all the places they took me were just a dream. After having an amazing time at the bar with my three sexy friends, I was speechless as I entered the hotel room.

I touched the card to the sensor to switch the lights on and the blinds started coming up automatically, as The Shard is just a wall of glass. All of London was in front of me. What an amazing view. I approached the glass panel.

'Oh my God, does money buy happiness?' I said to Mr Handsome.

He approached behind me and said, 'Personally, I don't think so. But for sure, it makes life so much more fun and an awful lot easier than being poor. I don't know anyone who prefers being poor.' We both giggled.

I was standing facing the glass and watching the city. London was at my feet. Looking at this wonderful view, I turned to Mr Handsome, who was still behind me, and I gave him a big smile and said, 'Thanks for everything.' I undressed myself right there in front of the glass pane, pulling my dress over my head, while he approached me from behind, touching my naked body, me dressed only in heels. All the rooms even smelled posh, and there we were, fucking with all the lights from the city behind us. And there was a delightful breakfast in the morning!

18

When divorce happens, it is so difficult to begin again. The first feeling is one of failure, and a fear of being incapable; but then, when you realise you can walk on your own two feet, alone, you get used to the freedom and financial independence and it is so difficult to go back. And the more time passes, the more selfish you become – not in a bad way, but in terms of becoming individualistic, as you are used to having to think only about yourself.

This was the state of my life as I started the second year in my new career. When your kids have grown up and suddenly don't need your support anymore (if parents have the luck of having a good child, as I had), when they leave home and start their own lives, then is the moment you realise that the only thing left to do is look after your own life.

I woke up every day and organised my bookings, and I always went to bed very tipsy. A glass of wine became a bottle and it was my only companion when I closed the door on my last client. I was spending my time staying at my work flat, absent from my home and daughter, who was old enough to have her own personal life and friends. My clients became my world. I didn't go out and I didn't socialise anymore, as I was busy most evenings attending to my bookings. I forgot what it was like to meet people and have fun for free. I kept my distance from the world. I never shared intimate messages with anyone. I only messaged clients if it was regarding a meeting. Suddenly, my private phone become empty and my work one was buzzing and busy twenty-four hours a day.

How difficult it was to be strong when a client became a regular and we shared intimate conversation, to not to develop a closer feeling and an attraction. If they claimed to be single, it made it so hard to avoid the impulse to call and invite them to go out. I needed to remember who I was: a paid service companion.

Never offer love to an escort if you can't give it. Love was a thing that I didn't believe a sex worker could afford to have, and the loneliness was just something I had to learn to deal with.

In life, when we choose a job, or when we want to do something, there is a question that comes to mind: why do I want to reach this goal or make this choice? Is it only for the money, or because I enjoy it?

When I ask myself this question, my answer is both; I for sure didn't start this job to be able to afford expensive shoes or bags. My goal was much more.

I didn't enjoy the fact of having to do it every day. Sometimes I would wake up and have the normal feeling of not wanting to have sex, but my bills were very high. A studio flat in South Kensington, just beside the station and few minutes from Harrods, was very expensive, so I needed to make money, and so I felt forced.

I am a quite habitual person in my private life. I'd had one-night stands before, but I was never good at dealing with them, as I don't like changing sex partners. I believe that sex gets better the more you get to know the person.

I had so many clients who were just business connections with no personal attachment. I wouldn't contact them unless it was regarding a booking. But still, I appreciated them and enjoyed the sex more when it became frequent.

I am still always nervous when I open the door to someone new and, have tried to build my client list to address these feelings.

In my adolescence, I was a very thin, shy girl. I had a very rigid childhood and had always to refer my dad as 'sir'. I had trouble expressing my emotions, so I used to put everything on paper, and now, after seven years doing sex work, I have the same need to write, to have a voice. It is very difficult, because English is not my mother tongue and I'm not a writer. I'm just a person who would like to make a difference because I see a very dangerous system denying sex workers the right to a voice and to defend ourselves.

I want to show people that this job does not only have a bad side, as everyone thinks. It is just another way to make a living. Not an easy one, but a fast one.

I am trying to open people's minds to not see it as something so wrong. I keep trying to convince myself that I am not ashamed, but I keep my secrets to protect my daughter, as I don't want to expose her. I will never show the face behind Lily and I don't tell anyone about what I do for the sake of my daughter. By hiding myself, I protect her, though she is already an adult. What worries me is that her friends are young and those sorts of young guys are on my website. Encountering one of them there is my biggest fear. But perhaps this fear is not only about her. It is also about the fear of judgment.

I suppose not many girls have the same luck and mentality that I have. The money made within the sex industry is very fast, but far from easy. Sometimes, it creates a toxic environment and, slowly, it takes a piece of us. It is tricky. You can achieve something, or it can be destructive, especially when you start to see a man only as a source of income.

Most girls see clients only as a sum of money, but I think it is about giving and receiving. Treat others as a number and you will become a number. And I don't want that with my clients. Not me. Working in Central London was the first time I had met nice and intelligent people and stopped struggling to the end of the month. I really wanted to enjoy, appreciate and get the most out of it. I didn't need a man to pay my bills.

When I had the idea about writing my memoir, my idea was to share my experience to give people a chance to see a different point of view, and, perhaps, change their own views and mentality in the same way I've changed mine. It is so important to view legalisation in the right way. This is the oldest work in the world and it is not going to stop. But safety is necessary for everyone.

In this country, exchanging money for sex is not illegal; brothels and pimping are crimes, and two girls in the same apartment are considered a brothel, when, for us, it is just about being safe and having the lowest costs possible. That way we're not alone and vulnerable to unwanted clients making unwanted visits. It is so confusing because being alone inside a flat brings vulnerability and it can be dangerous.

Another point: Imagine you are a young guy who goes out, has some drinks with friends, spends all night paying for the drinks of a few girls, who end up only letting you down. You don't want to go home, so wouldn't it be easier just to jump in a cab with your friends and go to a brothel, where it would be safe if it was legalised, rather than go to a private place, in the middle of the night, blind, where you don't know if the girl is really independent or if there are thieves around waiting to rip you off?

A legalised brothel is a place where you can just pick a girl you like and finish the night with a happy ending, and it's of low cost for people who can't afford an expensive girl. There's nothing wrong with it. It's just like going shopping; your wallet decides whether you can afford Harrods or Primark.

It is the same as in a club, but instead of paying for drinks all night and ending up alone, you go for a sure thing. You pay and you get, instead of looking for an independent 'escort' who doesn't even give you full directions when you are already tipsy and trying to find a half-given address.

What is safer? Having a pimp? I've never wanted one, and I've been lucky, but many times I've felt I needed one for security. It is not necessarily a bad thing; it all depends on how you handle the situation.

Clearly, he would work for me, not me for him, and I don't think there is anything wrong with that. Working for Fernanda, I would have been happy if she hadn't got involved with the wrong people and wasn't using drugs. I've never visited a real brothel in my life, but I saw a few in Germany and Amsterdam.

Here, I know a few girls who work in that way. Honestly, it doesn't look like a nice environment (anything that is illegal doesn't have a nice environment), but no one seems be forced to do that work. Not in most of the cases I've seen, especially in this country.

Some girls are not capable of working alone, like Fernanda. And then they end up in the wrong hands because of a bad legal system and their vulnerable personality.

Sex exploitation, work exploitation, physical exploitation, marriage exploitation – exploitation is exploitation. It is when the weakest side allows the other to commit abuse, and it doesn't really matter in what environment. It is about a mental or financial state in which someone accepts being manipulated, for so many reasons.

At the end of the day, pimps, agencies, factories, or any other industry where money is made from other people's work, are all the same. It doesn't matter if it is physical work or sexual work; it is about the environment and providing the right conditions for any type of worker. Anything illegal is swept under the carpet and is harder to control.

19

The sex industry is full of very well-paid jobs, where there is a high flow of money and prostitution, in most cases, is tax free. The question is: what generates pimping abuse?

When trafficking happens, we need a system that is ready to help and act severely against it. It doesn't matter in which industry it is. It is against the law to keep anyone working as a slave or by holding their passport.

When a pimp brings a girl here without permission to work, it leads to this situation. Yes, there are those who arrive kidnapped, against their own will, ending up in clandestine houses, having their passports withheld and their families threatened in their home countries. Those girls end up being physically and mentally abused, regardless of whether it is sex work or work as a delivery person, a kitchen porter, or in a food factory. Those people who traffic must be punished and the victim must be supported.

There are others who arrive with the promise of modelling jobs and end up with no modelling but in an escort agency. I doubt most of them are forced to do it; many discover how good the money is in this business and chose to accept the work, taking the profit from it. I wouldn't call those girls trafficked.

And there are those like me who just made the choice to change their lives and discover their sexuality. I chose not to have many clients, but quality ones, because I want my work to last long-term, but there are others who come into sex work for a very limited period and have around ten clients in a day, if they have good demand. A brothel is the perfect place to reach many clients in a day, so many girls end up doing a fast pace to get quick money.

This situation doesn't make a worker the victim of a pimp, but rather the victim of the hunger to make money quickly and to make a difference in one's financial life in a very short time. It is temporary, because if it is done in the long-term, pushing the body so much and so often can cause the need for drug use.

Money is a number and we when start to count, it never ends.

In the right brothel, especially in other countries where it is legalised, girls can choose the days they work, don't pay for rent and don't answer the phone, as they have a secretary to do the bookings. They pay their taxes and contribute to a pension. They are not alone, either. If they are not happy, they can just walk away and find another job, although one where the money would be much less. If they get abused, they can call the police.

It is just a matter of choice. It's a business like any other. They give a percentage of their income to the brothel and have their bills paid and their back covered.

Guys who can't afford to pay an independent girl in a nice flat, for one hour or more, desperately try to get fifteen minutes. I feel sorry for them because not having money doesn't make anyone a good or bad person. A good flat in Central London is very expensive, though. To make a decent money, doing fifteen minutes, I would need to take five bookings a day. It means five men knocking on my door. I couldn't do that as the price of my flat is too high to risk it and I don't want to use my body at that level anymore.

We independent escorts face another big problem: should we rent a place to work, or get a hotel room? Otherwise, where are we supposed to work?

This happened to one of my escort friends and it almost happened to me. After you pay the deposit and start renting a place, the agency finds out about your work and, very frequently, they are clever and come and ask you to move out, without any legal formalities. They keep the deposit and the girl leaves to avoid any problems.

I see brothels as a safe place and a route to fast money, if they are legalised and controlled by the police, and there was proper healthcare. Luckily, we already have a clinic I go to in Soho, where I am registered, and they are just amazing. The staff and the counsellors are so professional.

Dean Street Express is not a place just for gays. I've got a gold card from the clinic that shows I work in the sex industry, so they test me as many times I need, and every time I go there, the doctor, a lady who already knows me, comes to say hello and have a quick chat, to check if I need any counselling or if I feel safe in my environment. That clinic makes an amazing difference to us and the authorities and government should do the same.

Someone involved in politics told me once: 'Debating this argument is not interesting. It doesn't win votes in an election.'

'Well, but this means all the girls are being controlled and it's costing so much money in taxes, as so many girls don't pay,' I replied.

The government says that we need to fight against trafficking, abuse, blah blah blah, and doesn't realise how many ways there are to abuse a person. We need to stop the hypocrisy and start to see sex work as a job. There is a big hidden business behind it, and that should be unpacked.

I doubt that many girls are forced to do sex work in this country. It does happen, but I believe that there is more trafficking and abuse in food factories and with housekeepers and other businesses where the person who is abused is not visible.

Any man who pays to go with a girl can see if she is enjoying it, or if she has been forced. Clients are not monsters, or stupid, just because they are paying. Some are good and some are bad, the same as everywhere else.

It is more likely that a girl who is not allowed to work in the country and needs to make good money in a short time will do it, because she wants to change her financial situation or support her family. It is an immigration issue, not a human rights issue. So, women are most likely not forced to do sex work; it is a personal situation and choice, so let's to stop feeling sorry for these women. Not in this country.

I am the same as most immigrants, as I arrived here and didn't speak English. I had to adjust to a different culture and was working hard but not making good money. Working in a kitchen, waitressing, cleaning houses, doing hard work or getting married just so someone will support you is the situation of so many foreigners.

When I became an escort, I found that I could make much more in a week than I was making in a month at my old job, so that's definitely a factor for the many girls who choose this path. Now I am meeting nice people, creating boundaries, and I have found a new life – but this is probably not what many girls are interested in. They just want money. This is the difference between an escort and a prostitute; they are selling the same product, but at a different pace. I have done both and there is no right or wrong. It is just a choice.

For me, if all this was just about money, I wouldn't waste my time and the frustration of not having good English (even still, while writing this memoir). I could just keep choosing to do my job, selling my body, not worrying about who I was meeting, with guys who are only interested in me opening my mouth for other things than talking, making good money and being an invisible person, with no voice.

20

H*i Lily, hope you are enjoying the nice weather. Would really like to meet and come to see you. Two hours anytime from 4:00 p.m. onwards. Apologies for the short notice.*

What a nice message.

I opened the door and my face shone. A tall, well-dressed and handsome man was standing there. Perfect for a boring week.

He took a shower while I went to the kitchen to prepare the bucket of ice for the wine. There was the usual quick chat to break the ice and do the paperwork.

He was the Bite Man. He fucks. A lot and very hard.

Just starting to warm up, we kissed and, soon, he started to bite my lips, moving to my neck, breasts, down my body to my belly. It began a little mild, waiting for me to get warmer, watching how I was responding to his actions. He turned me around then, pressing me to the bed, his teeth drawn on my back. My neck got a big love bite and so did my breast and other parts of my body.

He stopped for few seconds to see my reaction, but kept going when he saw me enjoying it.

In rough sex, there two types: people who do it for dominance, and people who do it for violence. He was marking his territory, devouring my skin, and he knew how to bite. I could let out my submissive side with him. He took advantage of it and enjoyed it until he left me completely drained, my skin sore.

I am not a masochist, but sometimes, if I connect with a person, I do enjoy giving myself over to a bit of pain. It is very instinctive; just to be there, with the sensation of been punished, under someone's control. It doesn't happen very often and not with just anyone. That afternoon, I allowed him to do that, to abuse me.

The time flew, so we stayed there longer than planned. I didn't want him to leave; I was enjoying his presence. When I checked the time, I was already late to leave my flat to meet Mr Handsome.

I dressed to get ready for my outcall and he stayed there, watching and enjoying all my movements.

'I like different things and have lots of things to do with you, if you agree,' he said, following me with his eyes.

'Tell me about those things.'

'Another day, we don't have enough time today,' he replied.

When I was ready, he accompanied me downstairs. My cab was already waiting, so I got inside and carried on observing him walk behind the car, directly to the station. He had a faraway look, walking and looking at the sky, lost in his thoughts, so I kept watching him until the driver turned the corner, and I felt my heart tighten and start beating fast. I shouldn't have done it, it's one my rules, but I sent him a text:

Was so nice to meet you, thanks very much. You made me happy. x

I wasn't expecting a fast reply, as he would already have been inside the Underground, without a signal, but I got this response:

Oh, I'm the one to thank you. You made my horrible week disappear and gave me a time where all I could think was this feels great. So, you are a beautiful, naughty, angelic devil. I'm in your debt. Fantasy can't happen tomorrow as goodies won't arrive in time, but they will arrive soon and then maybe you will grace me as the lead in my little fantasy.

I was speechless, breathless, and I felt my face burning. I smiled. And then my phone died.

I got to the hotel bar, already tipsy, walking to meet Mr Handsome. I was very late.

'I've been stuck in traffic,' I said and Mr Handsome replied, 'I was worried, your phone was off.'

'My phone is dead,' I answered, realising that Mrs Kinky and the Fireman weren't there. I ordered my drink and asked, 'Where are they?'

'They will be here soon,' he said and the barman gave me my gin and tonic.

The Fireman and Mrs Kinky arrived a little while after that. She had a very relaxed expression, asking for a drink for both. 'Hendricks, please.'

'So, what have you guys been doing this afternoon? Anything special?' I asked. But actually, I feared asking this question of Mrs Kinky.

'We stayed in the room today,' she replied, I looked at her, surprised. 'But we had a guest,' she said, giggling, sitting beside me and opening her picture gallery to show me photos.

'We met a guy online and invited him to our room, as I fancied watching the Fireman fuck him.'

We all laughed at that. And then she showed videos of them.

This man had a big dildo, like fifty centimetres, and inserted all of it inside himself. I had already seen and done this kind of thing, but it was still impressive, especially coming from Mrs Kinky as, when I looked at her, I saw only a lady. I could never believe how pervy she was.

'I am supposed to be the kinky expert here,' I said, and we all laughed.

'Oh, this is nothing, Lily. I am going to the loo,' she said and directed the barman to give her a glass with only ice. She came back after a while with the glass filled and gave it to the Fireman, saying, 'Here is your drink, my dear. Drink that.'

Mr Handsome looked at her, amused, saying, 'No, you didn't just do that.'

'Yes, I did, honey; I am feeling very kinky today.' And she looked at the Fireman, giving him the glass. He drank all her fluid.

We just stared at them. 'Oh my God, she is my wife. I have no words,' was the only thing Mr Handsome could say.

In the morning, as had happened many times, I didn't remember a lot of things. I only saw my latex outfit scattered all around the room. It was Friday the 13th, so I had decided to bring it all. The bell rang and breakfast arrived. After having a long chat and some laughs, I remembered what had occurred the night before.

Mr Handsome looked at the marks and bruises on my body and asked me, 'And this?'

I told him about my meeting with the Bite Man. He loves to hear my stories. When I talk about my experiences, he gets turned on, and it worked with his wife, too. He can have an orgasm just from listening to sex stories. And while he was saying to me, 'That is why my wife is naughty. I just love it,' his cum spurted over him.

On my way back, I was tired, dying to get home, but I kept thinking about the Bite Man. How could I forget him when my body was this sore?

I went to my work flat, took off my shoes and clothes and fell onto my bed. I was knackered and felt like a truck had driven over my back.

I slept the rest of the morning and when I woke up, in the middle of the afternoon, I realised that my room was very messy from the previous day. I put my phone on to charge and started to clean. Two messages came through that I had missed last night. My face lit up with a big smile when I saw it was him:

I'll plan to come see you tomorrow, but the fantasy scenario is just as much about what I give as I what receive. So, for me to skimp on anything wild will only be me cheating myself and you. It will happen. I've been searching for you. I just didn't know it. ;)

Please forgive me for sharing or intruding, but I can't even remember the last time I was left being this horny after a session which I couldn't fault.

Wow. I was impressed with how this was working out. My panties were wet and I felt excited.

I thought it might be too late now, but I replied, anyway, as I had nothing to lose:

Don't ask me for forgiveness, I am very curious about your fantasy. Let me know if you are still up to meet me tonight.

A little later, he replied:

As much as I would love to, I can't make tonight as am at friends which I initially thought would finish up by 5ish, but looks to go much later. I hope you had as grand an evening as I did. Purely because of you and, yes, there were a few more hard times. I will be in touch for a night out. As long as everything goes to plan, it should be either Thursday or Friday. Geez ... I'm getting itchy just thinking of you.

Well, it was a great message to let someone down, with a sense of romance. It'd been a while since I'd had butterflies in my belly from nice messages like that, but in this lifestyle, we can't really dream. I am a sex worker, so there is no romance or nice messages. Maybe before the meetings, but almost never after.

21

Mr Black got back in touch, too:

Hi Hun, I have a potential booking for both of us on 17th, are you free? They are married couple, late 50's- will be at their hotel on Park Lane for ninety minutes. Massage for husband and wife to start then a little sex show (focus on wife).

Great, that is fine. Let's do that.

We rode to the hotel in a cab. He was a very friendly client, but she was a bit dry and found it difficult to let herself go.

It was not her first time to have a woman to play with her and it seemed like she was enjoying it, but we ended with Mr Black doing his job, using his big snake and his hand to see if she could squirt. She found it hard to get to an orgasm, but was getting there.

This was not his first time with her and it wasn't the last, either. The man was enjoying the show, telling me while we were drinking that they were not husband and wife. They were lovers. She was married to his best friend, but they had been seeing each other for a long time, cheating on the friendship as well as the relationship.

As his promised me, I received a text from the Bite Man on Thursday to invite me to the theatre on Friday, but the goodies hadn't arrived.

A cab left us at the Apollo Victoria Theatre at Victoria Station to see *Wicked*. I couldn't remember when I'd last seen a show.

We had a few drinks, enough to make me relax. It had been a while since I'd gone out in a kind of dating way. Afterwards we went to my flat and I opened another bottle. He walked over to my toy collection, picked up some handcuffs and arrested me.

After a long hour, we talked about domination games, BDSM and what he was more into.

Although I do lots of BDSM play, I usually am more dominant than submissive and my little secret was that I was a bit claustrophobic about being tied up, which is probably the reason why I was so attracted to ropes. The last time I wanted to be submissive for real was with Mr Difficult, and now I was intrigued and feeling very attracted to the Bite Man.

He asked me, 'Do you have any fetishes?'

I never talk about my real interests at my job because it would attract people who would love to manipulate me, as my weakness was the hope of finding the Alpha guy, the only one, and I would be there to please him outside of my business, in my private life. But I needed to make sure that he was the right one first.

He slept at my flat and we woke up and had a great fuck. My back ached though, and I still had a few marks from our first meeting, in addition to the new ones he gave me. But it didn't matter.

With each bite, there was pain that shuddered through my body, and when his teeth released the skin, the sensation of relief moistened my genitals. I was just so turned on by this man. He left in the early afternoon and I had to go home. I hadn't seen my daughter for two days.

'Wow, I am enjoying going out with him,' I said to myself, immersed in my thoughts, riding my lambretta home. I didn't see the car crossing the road. I swerved, falling onto the pavement.

I opened my eyes and saw two paramedics taking my blood pressure and, in the corner, I saw a police officer holding a little tablet.

'Hi, you had an accident and you lost consciousness. I need you to answer a few questions. Do you remember your name and your address?' one of the paramedics asked me. The officer checked my answers on the little tablet, saying, 'It's a match.'

The paramedic said, 'Seems all good with you. But, still, we need to do some exams,' and then, a few minutes after, I heard the noise of the ambulance. 'We need to take you to the hospital,' he said, and they put me inside.

At the hospital, the doctor did a scan of my body to ensure that I was OK. The only damage was a fracture to my foot, and I had my foot put in plaster.

While I was still lying on the gurney, I took out my phone and started to send messages, cancelling all my bookings, explaining to the clients what happened. Surprisingly, a few regulars still wanted to come and see me. One who I'd not yet met said, *I am really interested in meeting you, so if we can have a bit of playing and sex, I don't mind if you have a cast or can't wear high heels.*

It was surprising that someone would want to pay to see me with my foot broken, so I replied, *Oh, yes, sure we can play. I've been told by the doctor to keep my legs up*, and he sent a laughing face.

The client knocked at my door, and looked me up and down, smiling, as I was dressed in my nurse outfit, which is very short and open at the back with strips that show my peaches. I had a stethoscope around my neck, with my foot in a cast. I said, smiling, 'Ready for a check-up?'

He laughed. 'Awesome. You are so sexy.' The cast was not an issue and I gave him more than he was expecting.

Peter came to see me, as he was very worried about how I was. We didn't even play very much.

'Peter, don't you get tired of seeing me?' I asked him.

He smiled. 'Don't be silly, Lily, I will be your client until we are old and have walking sticks together.' It made us laugh.

How can I hate my job? At that moment, I realised who I should really be appreciating, as I was expecting a few regular clients to visit, but they just wished me good luck.

It had been a while since I'd heard from Jim, my toy boy. I sent him a few messages, but he was ignoring me. I sent another one:

Hi Jim, haven't heard from you, hope you are OK. I just had an accident and got a cast on my foot, just wanted to hear from you.

Five minutes later, my phone rang. It was nice to hear his voice: 'How are you? I apologise for not being in touch, I have been so busy.'

'Are you going out with someone?' I asked him and he gave me a little laugh.

'A few months ago, I met up with an ex-girlfriend and we started dating again. Sorry I ignored you, I realised I only want to be with her.' We had a good chat and I told him that she was a very lucky woman.

I kept fearing that suddenly one day I would realise that sex only meant money to me, so I liked the idea of having someone outside of my work, without the money exchange, to make me feel that men are not only a business. Jim had been my escape for two years and now I needed to find a new friend.

I have my personal requirements. I am picked by clients from this huge web catalogue, so I also want to pick someone who I like, and he has to be single. I want to be allowed to text and send messages and spend the night with them. I need a good friend with benefits. In the life I have, I cannot expect to have a man for myself because I am not that kind of woman, but I still need someone with whom I can be myself, and not feel like a working girl.

I was expecting a message from the Bite Man, inviting me out again, but, instead, I got a message saying, *I have a family bereavement and I'm at the airport on my way to my country.*

I need to replace Jim and he might to be the one, I thought.

I had my cast removed, but I was still using an orthopaedic boot and crutches. Luckily that didn't bother my favourite client, Mr Handsome.

We set a meeting up in a pub near Horse Guards Parade, where we were going to see a demonstration of the army, and the Queen would be there.

Bring all your toys, we are going to have play after that, Mr Handsome texted, so I filled my bag with dildos and toys.

They were already at the pub when I arrived and we had few beers before going to the venue. The weather was chilly and drizzling and my face paled when I saw all the security we would have to go through due to the presence of the Queen, such as X-rays and inspections. It made the situation very embarrassing.

I passed through the X-rays, then security opened my bag and, when he saw all my toys, he passed it to the guy beside him, saying, 'You inspect it.'

The second guy looked inside and passed it to the others. 'It's for you.' They were giggling, but they gave me back my bag.

Mr Handsome had no embarrassment, though.

'We will have fun later tonight. You guys are welcome to join us.'

Oh my God. I wanted to disappear. He was shameless.

I'd never seen him whine in the cold, but that afternoon, he was shaking and fatigued with the temperature. 'I am not feeling good. We are leaving in a bit,' he told me.

'We can go now, if you want. I am bored anyway,' I replied with a worried smile. He nodded in agreement, but Mrs Kinky and the Fireman stayed. We jumped in a cab and went to the hotel.

It was the Park Plaza in Westminster Bridge, where there were many guests from this event. All that embarrassment and then no play! He was not in the mood. He was very pale, but told me he was just tired, and had lots of work stress. We just relaxed, but I had never seen him like that.

22

Mr Adan was an important man – a diplomat – and he lived on the French Riviera. He was in London and came to knock on my door; I was flattered that he wanted to meet me.

He was very polite with the excellent manners that make a woman get very aroused. His wife had a brain tumour and the treatment meant that when she tried to have an intercourse, instead of pleasure, she felt pain and dryness. So, because of his job and the fact that he travels a lot, she made the clever decision to allow him to find another woman to release his sexual needs, but with the condition that they must be a sex worker, not a lover, so there was no attachment and no one from the town where they live. Also, she promised to never check his phone or his emails, as she doesn't want to know anything. And so, he did this and he has been my client for a while.

Tonight's meeting with Mr Handsome was at the Edition Hotel.

I arrived at the bar and the waiter gave me my gin and tonic. Mr Handsome was a bit nervous and gave me a peck on my cheek, instead of my lips, saying, 'There are a few people in this bar who I know, so we need to be very discreet. Stay beside the Fireman.' We were already a bit stressed because we were going to have a special guest.

Mrs Kinky kept beside her husband and they went to have a quick chat at another table. Then after, we had few more drinks. The Fireman stayed beside me, pretending he was my boyfriend, and slowly, we chilled out.

Trying to ease the atmosphere, I said to Mrs Kinky, 'You would be a great mistress.'

And she looked at me and smiled. 'If ever my husband goes broke, I would definitely run a dungeon.'

With lots of laughter, Mr Handsome said, 'Happily, I am not broken yet. Just imagine, how naughty would my wife be as a mistress?'

And I said to her, 'I am sure he is a successful man, but you would be a legend.' And we all laughed, toasting with a drink.

Then the Fireman got the message that our guest had arrived, but we needed to be discreet. I didn't know yet exactly who it was. He went out to escort her to the room. Mr Handsome and I left separately to not risk people see us taking the lift together. Mrs Kinky gave me the key card and I went on my own, while they left the bar holding hands.

I opened the door and I was breathless. She was beautiful. An amazing ladyboy.

Apart from Ash, the hermaphrodite, I never been with a transgender person, as usually they are very straight. I love them, I don't have any problem, but I am not their type. And Mr Handsome knows that I am very into it.

He arrived a few minutes later and we started with more drinks. To help her relax, we ordered a bottle of champagne, and then the play started.

She spoke very poor English. I approached her and she told me, 'No kiss please.'

Well, that was like an ice bucket going over my head. I started to try to make her more excited, but her expression was just indifferent and her head was somewhere else.

I asked, 'Are you OK? I am also a worker, so we need to please him. He wants to watch us to get turned on and then he will join us.'

She just said, 'I don't like women.'

'OK, so you go with him. He will play with you.'

'Oh, no, too big cock.'

'What?' I was already irritated. 'No, he is not big.'

Mr Handsome's sense of humour intact, he chimed in, 'Thanks for the comment, Lily, very kind of you.'

So, I grabbed his dick and sucked a bit to make it hard, then stuck it into my butt, saying, 'See? It is not too big.'

Mr Handsome said, 'Oh, yeah, thanks again. Maybe we should send her home.'

So he paid her and I was so annoyed about the £600 useless booking. Complete rip off. But he did not want to risk any problems.

My eyes widened, I felt butterflies in my stomach when I opened my phone and read a message I'd just received, with an invitation to the theatre. Bite Man was back in London. I felt more excited when he asked me, 'Can you wear a dress with a tall neck?'

'Sure, I will.' I wondered what the next surprise would be.

He arrived at my place at 5:00 p.m. and the show started at 6:30. He entered, giving me a kiss, touching my back, his hand sliding down to my butt, which he gave a pat. He discreetly placed the money on the table as usual, which I never count or take away, and went to refresh himself, as he had come straight from the office.

'Your gift has arrived,' he said as he came out from the shower, wiping his head with a towel, then opening his bag and giving me a few packages. It was a PVC outfit with chains up to the neck – this was the reason for the tall-necked dress request.

'Can you wear that under the dress, please?' he asked me.

Then, in another box was a plug to insert inside me. It was a vibrator that you can control with a remote control or via an app, even if you are in another country. A very interesting toy. He asked me to wear it for all our time out, imagining what a naughty night he was planning to have. I changed my clothes, inserted the plug and we left for the venue, already tight on time.

He enjoys musical shows, and this one didn't lack beauty in the performances. We were both having so much fun that I almost forgot what I had inside, until he took his mobile out and started to use it. I was thinking he was texting someone and I found that very rude, but I did not say anything, when suddenly I jumped up from the seat.

That thing in my pussy started to vibe inside me and I got very nervous. Then he slowed it down so it vibrated a bit more gently. He was laughing. I looked at him, gesturing about what was going on, and he beckoned me to be quiet.

He put his finger to his lips, but he was smiling. And he kept playing, up and down, until I had an orgasm right there.

I was sweating and even forgot what the play was about. I beckoned him to stop. The show had a break, so when the lights switched on I looked at him and asked, 'Are you having fun?'

He smiled. 'Yeah, a lot. I think you need the toilet, while I go for some wine.'

We left the theatre and I was amazed and happy, apart from the fact that my foot was still a bit sore from the accident. We got a cab back to my flat. I opened the door and went to the fridge for more wine, but when I entered the room, he just grabbed me from behind, very rough, and threw me on the bed, saying, 'I really enjoyed today.'

He loved chains as well and he still had one last surprise. It was a metal bar to spread my arms and legs. He tied me up in that thing and abused me all night.

After spending twenty hours together, all I wanted was that our time together would never end, but he jumped up to shower and leave. I got up, took the money from the coffee table and put it inside his wallet.

He finished getting ready to go and picked up his stuff, but then he noticed the money inside and said, 'Are you sure?'

I replied, 'If you want to see me outside of my business, yes, I am.'

23

Saturdays and Sundays are my days off, so I was back home with my daughter. But I ached all over, I could barely walk, and my legs were feeling very tired. I made a coffee, took two tablets of paracetamol and cancelled my bookings for Monday, with the excuse of having my time of the month.

On Monday, I went to the doctor, because my feet were very swollen – I shouldn't have been wearing high heels while I was recovering. In the afternoon, my daughter and I went to the supermarket and spent the night cooking and enjoying the moment. She doesn't talk much about my work or ask any questions, usually.

'How are you doing? Are you safe where you work?' she asked me, and I told her, 'Yes, I am meeting new people, and, honestly, I am really enjoying it. Clients have been taking me to nice hotels and it is really flattering be in such fancy places.'

'Oh, yes, much better than to go there to do cleaning,' she answered in a sarcastic voice, which surprised me.

'Do you feel uncomfortable about it?' I asked her.

She gave me a hug. 'I am still processing it. But you are my mum, you are free, I know you do it for us and I will never have the right to judge you. I know exactly how hard it was for you to support me. I still remember when we came to London and you struggled so much to pay the rent, to not live in a shared house. And I still remember when you used to eat the end of the bread for breakfast so I could have the middle and our lunch was half of a cheap pizza and pasta for dinner. How would I dare to judge you? No, I am proud to have a beautiful mother. I have many friends at school who have both parents, but others have single parents, and so many have issues inside their family. We don't have those. We live in a peaceful environment.'

I burst into tears.

I was planning to spend a few months with my parents, as their old age was coming on and they would not be here forever.

My dad's memory had already begun to fail and I needed to be with them for a while. Mr Handsome came to visit me at my flat for the first time. We had become much closer to each other, but, lately, he had been much quieter than usual and our encounters had been much more 'normal'.

'Your apartment is very small!' was the first thing he said when he came in.

'Oh, dear, how rude you are,' I said, smiling and giving him a kiss. 'I got some Diet Coke with vodka for you.' (He so loves that drink.) And I walked to the kitchen for some ice.

'I am not renewing my lease here; I'm thinking about getting another place when I come back from my holiday,' I said, giving him his drink.

'My wife wants to go for a week to Abu Dhabi for shopping. She wants to take Fireman and I'd like to meet you in Rio de Janeiro. You up for it? We'd need to leave on the same day – we're telling the kids that we're going on holiday together.'

'Yes, of course, that would be fun. Can we go to do hang-gliding?' I asked him, excited, like a child asking for a sweet.

'Of course, we will. Everything you want. Send me a message with the airport you want to fly from and I will book you the flight. We need to arrive at about the same time.'

The Bite Man and I went to the cinema. My daughter also decided to come, but watched a different movie with her boyfriend. She didn't like the fact that he left me bruised.

I arrived a bit late and met him in the lobby of the Westfield shopping centre. He buying some popcorn and hotdogs for us. I had given up my flat by this point, so we went to the first hotel nearby and enjoyed a calm night, without biting, and, in the morning, we sat in a little coffee shop near the station to have breakfast.

The next morning, I went online to find a place to work until my travel date. There was this aparthotel, not far from my flat, in Chelsea. I had already heard about it – a place where, even if the client knocks on the wrong door, they still win. It was full of girls.

I chose it because it's a big building, with around five hundred apartments, easy to book, and full of working girls. At night, I noticed a few guys smoking outside of the building. I reckoned they were pimps or maybe friends.

My last booking sounded very interesting. Mr Black had this couple who wanted to meet me at the Hilton Hotel in Park Lane. Dan and Claire.

I met them on the top floor of the hotel at the 10° Sky Bar, which had a beautiful view of Kensington. They were already waiting for me with a bottle of champagne. We introduced ourselves and had a drink to break the ice. Then we went to the suite.

Mr Black didn't come, but Claire had enjoyed him the night before, while her husband watched. Now it was the other way around, as it was her turn to watch her husband tie me to the bed.

She just watched, sitting on the sofa. Dan had the ropes ready. He tied me to the bed and started to play with me and give me oral. I whispered, 'Put your finger in,' and he did. I exploded, squirting all around. Judging by his face, I thought it was probably his first time seeing or making a woman squirt. He got very into it, but his wife couldn't keep watching.

'I think that is enough,' she said.

'I let you finish last night,' he retorted.

She put her head down and he went to her and they exchanged a few words. He came to me, saying, 'I am really enjoying it, but it's better if you leave.' And I left.

The day after, I got his text, apologising:

We are trying to get over a marriage crisis; pushing our boundaries, measuring our tolerance of seeing ourselves with someone else.

They had been separated and now they were trying to reunite, punishing themselves by watching the other having intercourse with strangers. I was thinking this while I read the message and replied, *I don't think that is a good way to heal anything.* There was no reply. 'When am I going to learn to stay quiet?' I said to myself.

It was my last day to meet Mr Handsome before my trip. We went to the Mondrian Hotel and had dinner at OXO. After dinner, we went to the rooftop bar at the hotel. I had invited my friend to join us. She was very beautiful and I wanted to see if he liked her, so he could call her to go out while I was away. We ended the night in a swinger's club. It was her first time at that place.

The mornings are the only time when we are sober. 'I am a bit overweight, but will put on more on this holiday,' I said, already worried.

He replied, 'OK, let's make a bet, maybe it stimulates you to watch your food.' He was already suspicious of my inability to close my mouth. 'I will pay you £5,000 if you lose five kilos on your holiday.' Obviously, he knows how much I love eating and being with my family would make it almost impossible. 'A thousand pounds for each kilo? Not bad,' I replied, laughing.

Two days were left until my trip and I met the Bite Man at Tottenham Court Road station, where he had booked a hotel for our last meeting, Before that, we went for dinner at a Lebanese restaurant near there and he made sure to give me a perfect farewell.

The room was simple, but large. There was a bathtub where he prepared a bubble bath. He put me in it and said, 'Do not get out until I tell you,' and he went to the bedroom, leaving me thinking how full of surprises he was.

I closed my eyes, letting the hot water with rose essence relax my body, lost in time, not knowing how long I'd been there. Later he came in, holding a bathrobe, helping me to put it on and taking it off when we got to the bedroom. He was already getting the ropes to tie me up and the whip that I gave him. He used to whip me because I liked it, although he preferred to bite.

To not feel guilty, he satisfies me first. After doing everything he knows I enjoy, then it is the time for his enjoyment. The more he treats me well, the higher will be the price that must be paid. He must mark his territory, and this time, he exceeded himself. He absolutely punished me with no limit to his hunger to devour my skin. He was starving.

I left the UK for my holiday and, a month after, Mr Handsome and Mrs Kinky left Heathrow airport. She got on a first-class flight to Abu Dhabi, and in the seat next to her was the Fireman, with his bright smile, already waiting for her. Meanwhile, Mr Handsome made his way to Rio de Janeiro, and I, on another flight, went to meet him there. Copacabana, here we go.

I got off my flight and he was already there, waiting for me with a chauffeur. We went to the Copacabana Palace Hotel and, on Sunday, he booked a helicopter to take us to the F1 in São Paulo.

Back in Rio, we visited a few places, and, finally, we went hang-gliding and enjoyed the view from the top of that wonderful city. Afterwards, during dinner at the hotel, he asked me, 'How is your diet? You are supposed to eat salad if you want those five thousand pounds.' Obviously, I had not lost any weight. 'I promise I will!' I said, after a week as a princess.

The week ended and the chauffer drove us to the airport. We had dinner and said goodbye. We would next meet in London.

24

I don't come from a rich family and, when I was very young, my parent's relationship was not going well, so my dad got a work offer and went to Japan, his home country. It was a kind of a break for both of them, but it was hard for me to accept.

A year after that, I had my heart broken by a boyfriend, so I decided to leave my country to join my dad. I wanted so badly to be close to him. I think, in my mind, I was also expecting to convince him to go back to my mum. So it was very disappointing when I joined him and found he was already with someone else.

My dad was a racist, which made him hard to talk to, so my older sister and I never really had a connection with him. He didn't allow us to have black friends. I remember that once my sister had a black boyfriend, and he did not talk to her until she ended the relationship. Those behaviours made me so angry, but he still was my dad, and I loved him. I was expecting, when I was in Japan, to be a part of his culture. Inside, I was hoping to understand a bit more about what made him tick and to bond with him for the first time.

He was dating someone, even though he was still married, and on my arrival he made me lie to everybody, including all his friends and his girlfriend, who thought he was divorced. He introduced me to her. She was a very friendly biracial woman of black descent.

'Do as I say, not as I do,' was my dad's law.

I found out he was a different man in Japan – great with his friends, a happy and open-minded person. But, at home, he was a very strict parent. Back in my country, he had cheated many times on my mum and she accepted it, but did not really forgive him, I guess.

My dad was a heavy smoker and a few months after I arrived, he had a stomach bleed caused by a major ulcer and ended up in hospital. When he left the hospital, he had to cut the cigarettes and go on a strict light and healthy diet. He was so miserable. I still remember him being in tears that night, when I cooked for him and he looked at the food with disgust.

'This is a pig swill,' he said and pushed the food away, so hard it almost ended up on the floor.

'You are sick, you need to eat that and stop the cigarettes,' I said, feeling incredibly angry. I raised my voice, as I was not happy with his behaviour.

'I'd prefer to die,' was his response.

I was already losing all patience, so I stood up from the table, and left, screaming, 'So, die then!'

I never accepted his girlfriend and the reason was not because of her skin colour, but because of my mother. That night, I was crying desperately because I could see that they loved each other, but, as his daughter, I only wanted her to get away from him.

In the morning, I made the hard decision to go see her.

'He doesn't eat what I cook and he has been so stubborn. Last night, he threw away all his food. You know why I don't accept you, but I desperately need you.' It was hard for me to tell her that.

'Please let me help you. I want to come and look after him,' she told me.

Soon after, she moved into the house and I left. I was dating a guy and moved into his house.

My dad wasn't the father that I dreamt of, but, in his way, he was a good parent. At sixty-five-years old, he had an old-fashioned mentality, very bossy and extremely strict; but, with his new lady, he found a bit of happiness.

It took a while to accept it all and talk to my dad, but as I saw that he was in better shape and much happier, I eventually accepted his situation and became closer to his girlfriend. But my heart always carried a knot inside it, which never cleared.

After a year, my mum decided to come to visit us with the purpose of finding out what was going on. She wanted to take my dad back to Brazil.

Her decision to come made everything very turbulent. My dad decided to take a month's holiday and obviously it did not please his girlfriend.

The day my mum arrived, we went to the airport to pick her up and that moment of facing her and us all hugging was, for me, horrible, as I had to pretend that everything was OK. Again, I was angry at having to lie, but my dad had promised me that we would take her to visit the country and tell her the truth.

But, instead, my mum asked him to come back. If he refused, she would ask for a divorce and live her own life. She'd find another man, probably, taking my younger brother and sister with her, and Dad would never go back home.

He had to make a choice. She gave him a month after her departure to decide. My dad chose his family. He was a coward about telling his wife the truth, and he left the woman he loved to go back to his family.

I was already an adult, so I never went back to live near my family. Months after my dad went back, my mum found a letter from his girlfriend. She had already suspected something, but now she had confirmation.

Despite all that, they are still together. My mum accepted my dad back, but she never experienced true forgiveness in her heart, so my dad's life has been full of demands and he never found happiness again.

Now, after over twenty years, they were old and my dad was still having health issues. I went to visit them at least three times a year. I supported them financially and I tried to get closer to them. My dad had no idea where my money came from and, if he did, he would frankly prefer to die and would never talk to me again.

I told him that my partner was extraordinarily rich, as they once saw Mr

Handsome in a video chat and I introduced him to them as my boyfriend. That was what they believed and they've never asked me if I was with Mr Handsome for money or love. Dad was proud of his daughter having a rich boyfriend, which seems so hypocritical to me.

For me, doing all these things for my parents made me feel closer to them, but it was still so hard for us to use the words 'I love you.' I wanted so hard to tell them that, but I couldn't. I have never told my parents that I love them.

25

I landed in London on Christmas Day and I spent all week at home with my daughter, as I did not have a flat to work from.

Mike, who works with investors, was staying in London for business. I went to meet him at his hotel to spend the afternoon together. He was one of my few clients who didn't have any requests. We just enjoyed meeting and I felt he was a good friend; he gave me inner peace.

At some point, I went downstairs to buy some sushi and we had that in bed. With him, I didn't feel like I was working. I had been away for three months on holiday, which meant I was not working, so I wasn't having any sex. So that evening met some needs, as the Bite Man was not in London, and neither was Mr Handsome, who was still on holiday with his family.

I booked a month in the same hotel in Chelsea where I was before, as I needed to get back in action.

Hi sexy. It's Carmelo. I have been waiting for your return. I came to see you about a week before you left for holiday and had a crazy time PSE. Are you free this Friday? Love, Carmelo.

Carmelo is a man who has stayed in my memory. He was my age, married with two beautiful teenage daughters, but his wife had mental health problems and suffered from anorexia. He worked so hard to maintain the balance in his family, to be a good father and a strong role model for his daughters. Dealing with all these problems at home though, he was carrying a heavy load, so I was his escape valve. He was a guy who I would not think twice about dating if he was free, but, clearly, he would never leave the mother of his kids or put her in a care home.

After a long break, his big snake was very satisfying. Sex with him was very good and I needed to warm up for going back to work.

I had a new booking then from Tony, an Australian guy who wanted a squirting experience.

'I had a girlfriend in the past who made me very skilled at female ejaculation,' he told me.

'I can see that by your oral skills,' I replied.

There was more foreplay and, when I couldn't hold back, I pulled him against me and he penetrated me. He had perfect self-control and, after he orgasmed, I joked, asking him, 'Are you a sex worker too?'

He laughed, saying, 'No, I work in a hospital.'

The time with him was quite intense. When he left, I could feel my legs shaking and my body trembling.

A table had been booked on the top floor of a fancy Japanese/Brazilian restaurant with a great view of London, as Mr Handsome and Mrs Kinky were back from their family holiday and were celebrating their return, greeting another year full of fun.

'I lost five kilos,' I said, and he smiled as he brought out a £5,000 cheque, saying, 'Well done.'

It was just what I needed after a long holiday. After all that time away, we had lots of gossip to share, and Mrs Kinky asked me, 'Did you manage to find a flat for yourself?'

'Not yet. I would like a flat in Waterloo, as I would love to be there, but they refused me because I don't have enough income to rent in that area.'

To my surprise, she looked at Mr Handsome and said, 'What are you waiting for? Waterloo is a great location for all of us.'

He looked at her with a smile. They communicated without words, and then he told me, 'Text the number of the agency to my assistant on Monday and I will sort it out.'

After dinner, we jumped into a cab and went to the hotel. We arrived at the room and, bad luck for me, the toilet had a set of scales.

We were all tipsy, so Mr Handsome said, 'Come on, girl, let's check your weight.'

'NO! Did you ask them to put scales in the room?' I said, while he doubled over laughing.

'You are a cheat. Of course, you did not lose the five kilos. Give me back my cheque.'

I was trying not to give it back and we both fell onto the bed, laughing and fighting for the cheque.

'Jester!' he said, pulling at the cheque. 'I am not blind. I can see you did not lose all that weight.' He ripped the cheque while I was trying to hold onto it, hysterical with laughter.

On Monday morning, I sent the number of the agency to his assistant and, by the afternoon, I got an email from the agency with a contract. I could not believe it. The flat I dreamed of was now mine.

The day after, I met the agent in front of the building to get the key and, as a joke, he said to me, 'Your guarantor has a good job.'

I replied, 'Yes, and he enjoys collecting loads of zeros in his bank account.'

I couldn't believe that I had the key to an apartment in one of the best locations on the Southbank, close to Parliament and a short walking distance to Waterloo, the biggest station in London – a very strategic location.

I wanted a flat that was better than the one in Kensington. It was in a nice building and three times bigger than the previous one.

Again, I wanted my clients to come in and forget about the outside world. Low lighting, lots of candles and good decoration. And a big drawer full of my huge collection of toys. I'd have plenty of space for that now.

'Mum, what would you think if I went to live with my boyfriend? my daughter asked me. You have a nice flat and can live there.'

My heart was frozen. It was my time to realise that my kid had grown up. So, I decided to move into my new flat, leaving her alone, so her boyfriend could move in. The flat in Waterloo was bigger and more expensive, so it'd be a waste for me to only go there for bookings.

Since my baby was born, I had never lived alone. Wherever I went, she was with me. When I lived in different countries, she was with me. Living by myself, without my baby, felt hard and empty. I felt a big hole in my heart. I guess no parent wants their child to grow up. I taught my daughter to walk and now she could stand on her own two feet.

I cooked dinner one tonight, as Mr Bite Man was coming to visit me. I prepared the atmosphere, lighting lots of candles to warm up the flat. I was so excited as now I was by myself with him and he seemed so happy for me. We ended up breaking the bed in two pieces while we were playing!

I then got a call from my daughter's friend. They'd gone clubbing and my daughter had gotten very drunk.

'We are stuck near Trafalgar Square and she can't walk. All the cabs are refusing to take her.'

I said, 'Give me the location, I am coming.'

I got there and my daughter was sitting on the pavement beside her friend, half-conscious. He put her inside my car and she threw up while I drove her home.

In the morning, I left her in bed and went to a yoga class before going to my flat. She called me, crying and very depressed. I was sure she hadn't only been drinking, that she had taken some drugs.

I just said, 'Mum is coming.'

We spent all afternoon chilling, cooking and chatting, and we shared a bed. I stayed until she felt better.

'Do you think it's worth taking that shit when you are out?' I asked her.

'No, Mum. I did it because of my friends. They were all taking it and gave me some. I wanted to try it, but it is not a good feeling. I'm better off with just few vodkas with orange,' she said, with a miserable sick face.

My bad week didn't end there. I had another guy who booked me and then, ten minutes before, he texted me saying that he was on his way and he'd be with me on time and was bringing some coke for us. I got very annoyed, as my profile is very clear:

I am not a party girl. I do not meet guys for party or after party. Please, don't waste your time calling in the middle of the night when you are high, just because I have an interesting nickname. If you arrive at my flat stoned, don't bother. I am not a drama queen person. It is not my style. It is you who will waste your time and money. ['Party girl' is slang meaning that I share drugs. We cannot use the word 'drugs' outright due to the site's moderation policy.]

I did not think twice about telling him my boundaries. Taking drugs had become very personal, so I hated even to hear about it.

He arrived and, after he paid me, I went to another room and hid the money. He sat on the sofa, taking out his little bag of coke. I stayed where I was, just watching him, and when it was on the table, I said, 'Get out of my flat.'

He looked at me, annoyed. 'What do you mean?'

'I will call the police,' I said with a very serious face.

He stood up, about to argue, but he clearly realised I was not in a mood, so he just said, 'Can I have my money back?'

'Let me refresh your memory. My profile clearly says no drugs, so get out!'

He was so angry as he left, banging my door and calling me a 'bitch.'

'I know I am,' I whispered to myself.

The Bite Man took me out once a week and we spent a nice quiet time together.

This time it was my turn to surprise him about where we'd go to eat, and I choose a Brazilian restaurant. He loves meat.

'Can you put the toy that I gave you inside you?' he asked, giggling, and I did it.

During dinner, he played around by controlling it on his phone. It was actually very exciting, having all this feeling during a meal. It started out mild, so he was just teasing, making me horny and very wet.

'I need to go to the toilet,' I said and he stopped. I stood up and asked the waiter where the toilet was. He pointed downstairs. I walked down the stairs and needed to grab the handrail to not fall. The toy was vibrating inside me so hard that I felt it was going straight to my G-spot. I could feel my underwear was getting soaked while I walked to the toilet and I needed to use the hand dryer to dry my knickers. When I came back, we couldn't stop laughing. I was wearing jeans and, in the cab, he seemed very excited, wishing I had a skirt instead.

We got back to my flat and he was already very hard, asking me: 'How much do you like these jeans?'

I replied, 'Not too much.' So he ripped them in a second, giving me more bruises.

I felt hooked by him and was starting to suffer when he was not around.

26

Fetishes, fantasies, sadism, obsessions or mental disorders – we all might have them.

There is always something that turns us on to think about, and sometimes it is not even possible to control it; it can become an obsession.

I believe there is always a reason behind a fetish or fantasy, perhaps something that has marked your life. It could be a trauma which then leads to an obsession or mental disorder. Then, it is time to draw the line and decide if you require an escort or a psychologist.

When I became a sex worker, I had no idea how many people with different fetishes, requests and personalities I would meet. Stocking fetishes, latex, handcuffs, secretary fantasies, even crushing popcorn near your ear or smelling stinky shoes, and on and on.

Jack was my first slave with a foot fetish. He came almost every day and when he visited the flat, everything would end up spotless. He paid me to clean my room and would do whatever I asked him, and, in exchange, he loved to caress, kiss and adore my feet. I still don't understand how someone gets to that point, but, in his mind, it was the price to have me as his mistress.

My favourite transgression is crossdressing, which makes me believe that I want to hide who I am or cover my shyness. I feel extroverted and free when I am performing as a sex worker, but, outside, I am a simple and discreet person, meeting the acceptable standards of society in terms of being a good mother, apart from the fact that I am single.

My weakness during this time was being hurt by the Bite Man; carrying his marks on my body had already become an obsession. Do I carry any trauma? Perhaps I could be punishing myself for things that I regret, because when I am sad, I want to release it, so I feel like I've discharged all the negative energy inside my body. On the other hand, I don't think I feel any frustration about my past. It might just be a moment when I get to play hard and feel submissive, or push my boundaries even further. This was a new game for me and it was like playing with a new toy. I could see how he affected me.

George had a pantyhose fetish. He was a young Greek fella who requested me to be completely covered with stockings, including my face. Even if I was to drink, I had to keep the stockings covering my mouth. It was a funny feeling. With some scissors, he made a hole in the stockings, but only across my intimate parts. Then he laid on the bed, put me between his legs and contemplated me for almost forty minutes.

He contemplated my ugly face covered with the stockings, looking like a monster, caressing my face and lips softly. Then he put a leather collar on me and tied my hands, starting to play and use toys on me. I felt very interested and he was enjoying it, when I asked him,

'Are you not gonna fuck me?'

'Yes, I will. Oh, I will,' he said. 'I am not in a rush.' And he just kept playing with me.

What an interesting meeting, I have to say! At the beginning, I felt very odd, as it was such a strange request, but once the game was happening, I just got involved and turned on. Probably because I could see the pleasure on his face. Maybe he saw that fetish in some porn movie and wanted to try it, but he knew what he was doing and it made me to want to push my boundaries, too. We had a long chat after that. He was young, twenty-eight, and very handsome, but, as he said, it was hard for him to explain to a girlfriend this peculiar fetish, and I completely understood why.

'One to ten, how ticklish are you?' Alex, a young French guy, asked me, as he called to book me for thirty minutes of killing tickles, while I was tied to the bed. It was a half hour of torture, making me laugh so much I thought I'd die, with my stomach already in pain, while he laughed too, enjoying doing it. He never got naked and we never had sex, and when I asked him, he confirmed that sex wasn't going to happen. And it never did.

'How do I taste?' I asked Benjamin who came once a week to drink my fluids. I used to always eat pineapple before our meeting.

'You taste like a piña colada,' he replied.

It's hard to explain the number of times people have asked me to meet them in a public place or a bar to talk loudly about how small their cock is. Also, it was very common for people to ask me to do the role play of being an auntie or parent.

It is not my cup of tea. Although I have done it, I don't enjoy humiliating anyone or pretending to be your relative or your child. I believe the people who like that are probably frustrated or have experienced this kind of abuse. One of the signs is that almost all the people who have confessed to having those fetishes seem very unstable and sound very anxious, talking in a low voice. I had a few people who shared the abusive experiences of their childhood. In those cases, they really need a doctor, not an escort.

My main service became squirting and people asked so many questions about it, it started to feel like I was abnormal. But I am just a G-spot orgasmic, when most women probably get more stimulated by clitoral play. As to whether it is actually just urinating, I don't think so, in my opinion, but, in truth, this would be a long conversation.

I never crossed the line into hardsport, but I don't judge it. One day, I asked to a client, who was a doctor, what might be the reason people do that, and his answer was very simple:

'Why does a child love picking their nose and eating it? We don't know why and it is so hard to make them stop this disgusting habit. They just do it impulsively.'

When I watch movies that show people having sex in public places, I wonder if it is very exhibitionist, or do people just like it because they feel the danger? I have to say that I get really turned on by the idea, but I have tried it before and the fear of getting caught is so stressful that it makes me lose concentration completely. I leave that for swingers' clubs.

Good afternoon, I was just wondering if you would be interested in an early morning (8a.m.) meeting. This week on Tuesday? I'll be staying in a nice Kensington hotel but would be happy to come to you. I'm a mature guy who is well-mannered, respectful, very clean and open-minded. I enjoy giving anal and, although I don't like a strap-on, I do like my arse fingered. I also like to give good oral and I'm told I have a wicked tongue.

If you are interested in meeting for a couple of hours, drop me a line.

Gentleman Craig x

I read his message and replied:

Hello Craig. Is that next week? I am available and I would love to meet you to enjoy some A level play. You can contact me by text and, if you don't mind, you can place the booking request via the site. Looking forward to seeing you,

Lily x

Gentleman Craig used to regularly stay in Earls Court and had another stay booked for that week. I met him when I was still working in Kensington. Some of his obsessions were well-established by then, and one was anal sex. He fancied a meeting with someone new, so searched on AW, the website where I advertise, and filtered our escorts by location and A level. He scrolled down the list and there were quite a few girls, but one profile stood out: mine. The profile looked excellent and I had very good feedback, sharing all his likes, and it sounded within walking distance, so it was perfect and we soon arranged our meeting.

Early one morning, he walked down Cromwell Road from just a few houses away and rang the doorbell.

Gentleman Craig impressed me in every way. He was a very calm and gentle guy. We had a warm welcome, but what seemed like a normal meeting came to a very different end. He had brought something to introduce me to, but he was clear that if I was uncomfortable, we could just leave it and do other sorts of play.

He had brought a urethral sounding kit. Basically, it was a long metal device which you introduce into the urethra to get to the prostate via the penis. And if you are into such kinky things, it is impressive how pleasant it can be.

At first, I was very nervous and felt terrified of using it. But, after I saw him enjoying it, I started to relax and he told me that my hands were gentle, so there wasn't any problem. A few more glasses of wine and we started to relax.

After a while, he could see that, although I was still a little nervous, I was enjoying it, and he felt relaxed in my hands.

We met three more times that year, but then his visits to London stopped, although I did see him once more, in Stratford.

We moved on to some electrics and then the ball crusher, which had two clear Perspex plates with a screw that tightened until it crumpled the balls.

Gentleman Craig didn't get my regular client treatment; it felt like we had known each other for a long time.

Sometimes we'd exchange texts and emails, and I had the courage to ask him the reason why he liked genital pain.

He said, *The simple answer is, I don't know. I never really thought about it.*

Maybe it was a bit like my Bite Man?

He said to me,

I had a normal upbringing and have been with the same woman for thirty-nine years now, but I have always had obsessions. Drinking to excess (though I was never a drunkard or alcoholic), workaholism and, in my later life, women, sex and CBT. I believe that we all have these emotions, obsessions and wants inside us, but some are very deep and dark, and some people become extreme criminals through them and others become addicts of one description or another. Sometimes there's a very fine line between them. I'm sure there is an unlocking process for this in people and it requires the right person or a set of circumstances or events to do this for them. Or a combination of these. I also believe these can generally be conquered sometimes with help and sometimes with deep self-control, but it is not always the case. For me, my obsessions with women, sex, BDSM and CBT came much later in life. I'd always strayed a bit, but when the Internet and porn became so easily available, I started to watch more and more of it, and I didn't know or have the courage to seek it out for real until around 2010.

Now, Gentleman Craig is retired and, with that, he left behind the girls he used to meet. He left behind those kinky experiences to have a normal life near the beach. I asked him, *Why did you decide to retire and stop being with girls?*

For some time, I had been unhappy at work and decided to retire. It took some time to put everything in place before I set the date. I had many obsessions and decided to deal with all of them, except one. I decided to delete my AW profile, but needed to put something in place for my longest obsession. I found a tiny twenty-nine-year-old girl around ten miles from where I lived. She was eastern European, submissive and liked anal. She is a yoga teacher. I arranged to meet her and she was good fun. When I deleted my AW profile, it was a good feeling, a weight off my shoulders and I felt I had been set free. At the same time, I deleted every single contact, apart from a very few favourites. You are obviously one of those. Over the years, I had four hundred and twenty-nine meetings with various girls and could have bought a small house with all the money I spent. However, I have no regrets and I came across some fabulous people over this time. So far, I've not missed the old days and the dark obsessions are gone. The days of waking up thinking about my balls being stabbed, crushed, fried or pulled off have gone.

My monthly visits to my yoga instructor are going well and keeping me young lol. Maybe a trip to see you would have a better effect lol.

I wonder what it felt like stopping something that had kept you feeling alive and young during your life. I wonder when I am going to decide I have to stop, as it will be hard. I don't think it will take much longer for that time to arrive, but it will feel like a challenge.

27

Susy has a brown Latin body, as she's from Rio, with a big bottom and enormous natural 34F boobs, which make any man breathless as they're dipping between them. I met her before we started to do escorting, when we were working in catering, and we have been friends since then. I never wanted to work with her because we have a good friendship. This time though, I decided to give it a try, as she had been working for an agency, but the agency was just another brothel, really. We decided to do duos. It helped that her English was good, and she had the potential to be an independent and manage all her bookings on her own. She didn't have a flat to work in, however, so I invited her to stay with me for few days a week. It was safer and much more fun than being alone.

She was in a boring marriage with an office worker who travelled a lot; two kids and the stress of his work had made their sexual activity go down to zero. This was what made her dissatisfied and complain that her husband didn't see her as a woman anymore. When she was thirty-five and tired of relying on him for money, she ended up cheating, and then entered the escorting world a year after me, where she found that this life was a way to get back her self-esteem and sexuality, just as I did. She said that at least her clients loved and desired her to the point of giving her extra money. I completely share most of her reasons for doing this work, apart from the fact that I'm not married anymore.

Peter, the Swiss guy, was in London and, logically, he booked us both as soon as he heard about my new friend. I organised a threesome.

She was still getting ready when he rang the bell. He always brought a nice bottle of Chablis. This time, he brought three. He was fussy about wine and food.

He sat on the sofa before taking his shower, and, as usual, I had the ice bucket ready for the bottle. I opened it and poured some for both of us. He took a Viagra, which he swallowed with a sip of wine.

Susy opened the door in a very small dress, showing all her plus points. She gave him a DFK and his eyes were just staring, delighted by her breasts, which made him feel breathless with his face in the middle of them, just holding her enormous peaches.

Peter was a person who always made the night fly by, and we were very tipsy. This was Susy's first experience with a girl and the evening extended until late, leaving all of us exhausted.

The day after, she arrived at my flat, opened the door and came in with a miserable expression. She looked at me, very annoyed. 'My husband was so angry last night. I was enjoying it all so much that I completely forgot to check my phone. He tried to ring me so many times and I did not even think about it. He was so mad at me.'

'What did you tell him?' I asked her.

'I said I was out with friends, but he didn't believe me. Then we had a big argument and he was yelling at me and he asked if I had another lover.'

'So?' I kept listening in anticipation.

'So, I was drunk and I laid out everything I was holding inside me. I needed to let it out. I asked him, what did he expect, if he doesn't even touch me anymore?

'Then he said, "But you are still a married woman and I am your husband." So, I said I wanted a divorce.'

I was staring at her. 'What did he say?'

'I will never give you a divorce. I will never stay away from my kids.'

And then they went to sleep.

I hugged her, saying, 'Oh my God, imagine if he finds out exactly what you do?'

'I don't want to think about it,' she said, in tears.

Christmas was approaching and it was very busy during the last week before the holidays. Men like to treat themselves then. It's also very common for gangs of thieves to book girls to commit an assault, and it seemed like my flat was on their target list, as I had been receiving many weird messages. As I always speak to clients before accepting a booking, I heard some very odd voices and stupid questions.

Susy was still working with me. She was using my spare room and I felt much safer and less alone. We could have good time, even without clients, sharing a bottle of white wine. (She hates red wine.) I was only taking bookings from my regulars, as I didn't feel it was a safe time.

Susy had two bookings one day and, when she finished, she got ready to go home. We had a glass of wine together, and she left my flat around 10:00 p.m. But about an hour later, she rang me in tears, stuttering so much that I could barely understand what she was saying. One of the guys who had come me to see her waited for her downstairs with another two. They probably wanted to come to my flat, but got scared because of the good surveillance system in my building. So they waited for her, followed her, and when she got out of the Underground and walked to her house, they put a knife to her neck and got her bag. She was just 200 yards from her house and she was thinking of her kids. Her husband was travelling and the children were with a nanny. They committed a crime and risked her life for just £300.

Susy was traumatised. I don't blame her, as anyone would be who had a knife to their neck. After this occurred, she went a few days without coming to the flat and I tried many times to call her, with no answer.

She decided to come back and she had a guy who'd booked her. When she agreed to the time, he said, 'Thanks, I'll ask you the flat number when I arrive.'

She came to my room, looking concerned.

'Lily, I have this booking, but he hasn't asked for my address. And checking on my phone, I haven't seen him before. He is a new client. Can you check your phone? He might have been here before for you.'

I checked, but there was no saved number on my phone, either.

'Let's wait,' I said. 'If he comes, you meet him. I will be here inside my room. I don't have any more bookings, so, when you finish with him, tell him that you want to introduce me to him, in case he wants to change or do threesome. And let me deal with him.'

He arrived. I prepared a bucket with ice and a bottle of prosecco, and waited for them to finish.

I heard noises and, when he was walking to the shower, she came into my room.

'Yes, he is coming to see you.'

I opened the bottle, pretending to just be chilling and enjoying my prosecco.

They entered my room and she introduced me to him.

'Did you have good time with Susy?' I asked him, touching her breasts and smiling, while she sat beside me on the couch. (Clients love this scenario.)

'Oh, yes, she is nice,' he replied.

'She is gorgeous,' I confirmed, giving her a tongue kiss, already pouring some prosecco and giving it to him.

'How did you find the building? You didn't even ask her the address. Do you have any friends who have been here?' I asked.

'No, I read some reviews on a blog and the guy even told everyone where you both are, including the building name. I know this area very well. She has been popular and they talk about you both being here together.'

Oh, that blog, I thought. 'Are they allowed to share our location?' I asked him. I was very curious, but more annoyed. It is illegal for two girls to be working in a flat and these guys have been exposing me?

'Well, I don't know about that, but it is on there.'

I was so angry. I already had problems when the administrator ignored me before. I was feeling tipsy, so I decided to wait until the next day to sort it out.

The day after, first thing in the morning, in less than five minutes, I created a fake profile, but I still needed approval. A few hours later, I was welcomed as a punter and could read all the chit-chat about Susy and myself.

Oh my God. Many things on there were so funny, but many never happened. And my building's name was there and it was not fun to see that, as everybody who read it now knew where I was.

So, I went to the bottom of the page, where the terms and condition are given in a tiny font, and read it all. It stated that users were not allowed to reveal the place where a girl was working, unless it was a public space, which was not true in my case.

I reported the review, and the site asked me what I thought was wrong about it. I wrote that I was Lily and that the review showed the name of my building, which was against their terms and conditions. I added that the review was nice, so he could leave it, but delete the line showing my location, for our security. I also shared with him what had happened to Susy a few days before. I pointed out that it could make it easy for gangsters to find us, telling him how easy it was to be an anonymous punter on this site.

Hoping to resolve the problem, the day after, I tried to log in to see if anything happened, but the only thing I could read was

You have been banned from this site. It is annoying, isn't it?

My face was burning with anger. 'I only asked him to delete a line. How does he dare to do this?'

I tried to make another account, but my IP address was blocked, so I was stuck.

So, I went to my daughter's house and told her what happened.

'Let's make a profile on my computer,' she said.

She opened her laptop, as she was also so angry about it, and, again, she easily became a member. It took less than twenty-four hours. I clicked on the contact button and wrote him a little message:

Hi there, it is Lily again; I only asked you to delete a line of one of so many reviews about me and Susy; it is just a line and I was very polite; instead, you blocked my IP address.

I just want to make it clear that it is against the terms and conditions and, particularly, it is against my privacy. You ignored me, treating me as if I'm your property.

I want to let you know that, if you delete all my feedback, I would be happy, as it is against my will to be on your blog and I don't need your website to find clients; again, remember that I don't need you, but you? You need us girls to remain where you are.

And again, my daughter's IP address was blocked with the same message. *It is annoying, isn't it?*

That day, the administrator made a big mistake in ignoring me, because I could have seen his site as a powerful platform to grow my popularity, and I would have been willing to create scandalous scenes to attract more readers. But, instead, I repudiated their inconsiderate behaviour in confronting sex workers. Now I would do the only thing in my hands – apart from some clients who I already knew, I would not meet anyone who contacted me through that site, and I was going to make that clear. It was my way to boycott that forum.

Hi Lily, I have read so many nice reviews of you on the blog and I am interested in make a booking with you. Are you available by any chance?

I replied:

Hi there, thanks for the message. I want to let you know that I dislike that blog and it is against my will to have any good or bad reviews of me on there. There is nothing that I can do about it, except that I have decided to not meet anyone who is a member of that chit-chat site. Please, feel free to share this message with your punter friends and post it on there, you have my permission for that, and please do not take it personally. It is between me and the site.

Thanks

Lily x

The same week, Bobby, a foreign guy, booked me and when he arrived, I got suspicious.

He came in and he was very nervous. He looked around my room and I invited him to sit down and offered him a drink.

'No, thanks, I changed my mind and I want to leave.'

'That is fine, but I have this time free for you, so please accept a drink before you go.'

'No, thanks, I really want to go,' he insisted.

'No, you are not leaving now. We will have a drink and a chat first; you are here to check out my flat, aren't you?'

'No, I just changed my mind.'

I was firm. 'Then show me the money. I don't want it, but just show me that you brought the amount to pay me for the booking.'

His face went pale. He was so nervous, so I did not wait for a reply to tell him: 'See? You did not bring any money and the person who booked me on the phone had fluent English. You don't and it's not the same voice. I don't want any trouble and I think you don't either. I don't keep money in this flat. There are cameras inside the building and the security here are paid to protect the people who live here, not to question.' And then I gave him a very generous single malt and toasted him. He drank almost all of it in one gulp.

I looked to see his glass was almost empty and asked, 'Is that good?' He finished his drink and I said, 'Now it is time for you to leave.'

I closed the door and heaved a big, relieved sigh, but my heart was still pounding.

AdultWork, the website where I advertise, is very controlled, and us girls must deal a hundred percent with our own profiles: the writing, pictures, links ... everything must be self-made and we need consent if we want to post anyone else's picture in our profile. We are not allowed to advertise anything else on the page. If I post a picture of me and Susy, I need her written consent and they are very strict, penalising people with suspension, and you can be banned if you persist in breaking the rules. Even when clients write field reports about meetings, if we girls don't want people to read them, we can just cover them up. We are completely free to manage our own pages.

It is a catalogue of sex workers who offer services of their own choice, having full autonomy to manage their own images on their pages, and their privacy. While this site is controlled by the website monitors, on the other chit-chat website, punters post without any moderation. Well, they do have moderators, who are other punters, but they are just dying to have more and more field reports to satiate the hunger for more and more gossip, not caring about the welfare or rights of the sex workers. They have no clue. They copy private pictures from our pages of where we rent and post these on the blog, violating our rights. Because the chit-chat is not controlled, many guys end up becoming pretty toxic when talking about girls and pornography. They act freely and the site makes it easy for thieves to get information about sex workers. As I said before, I asked them to do one simple thing for the sake of my security and they just sent me a sarcastic message. Who should I call then? Isn't this just another way of abusing women?

28

I was looking forward to my birthday, when I usually take month-long holiday.

'Should we go on vacation somewhere nice to celebrate your birthday?' Mrs Kinky asked me while we were chatting at a bar.

'Wow, I would love to. Where?' I asked, smiling already and very excited. She likes to do big things.

'What do you think of having fun in Thailand?' she proposed.

'And some ladyboys?' I asked with a shining face.

'Of course! We will go in high style,' she said, looking at her husband and then to the Fireman.

Upon my arrival at the airport, Mr Handsome, Mrs Kinky and the Fireman were already there, waiting for me. It was my first time using a VIP lounge and I saw all this food and drink available, much better than waiting for a flight sitting beside so many people in the normal waiting area. We had a snack and, when it was near to our departure time, Mrs Kinky gave me her husband's passport and an envelope with money.

'He is yours from now on and your responsibility. Don't lose his passport and don't give him too much money. He will lose it.'

When we embarked on the plane to Thailand, we were escorted by agents from the airport – this was also my first time flying first class. We had spacious seats with a lilac orchid on each table and a flight attendant approached to welcome me, asking, 'Would like something to drink? Perhaps some champagne, Madam?'

'Oh, yes, please. Champagne sounds wonderful,' I said, stupidly, as I am not really a big fan of champagne. But it sounded so posh that I didn't care if I would have a headache after. It was all just like a dream. My birthday treats had begun and I was so excited.

We landed in Thailand and, again, were given priority in terms of immigration and customs checks. (Luckily, they did not open Mrs Kinky's luggage!) A driver was waiting to take us to the resort.

Pattaya is Thailand's paradise for sexual fun, and there we were, dying to play with some ladyboys. We relaxed for a bit in the suite and then went out to eat and explore the night.

Everything in Pattaya smells of sex. We went to this club where we saw very cute 'ladies' and started to drink. We were all very happy and excited. The Fireman was as fun as ever. After many drinks, we were all tipsy and surrounded by many girls. He jumped on top of the bar where the lap dances were and started to do a show dance.

Everyone in the bar went crazy, clapping and singing loudly and then, suddenly, he just took off his jeans; he was wearing a small G-string covering only his penis and he started doing a striptease. It was hilarious and all the girls and customers were screaming and laughing. He kissed my forehead, saying, 'Happy birthday, my dear.' Mrs Kinky kissed my cheek and then Mr Handsome. We made a deal then. Every night, one of us would choose who would end up in our room.

'Tonight, you pick one,' Mr Handsome said.

So, we started to look around and I spotted someone. She was stunning; she'd had her entire body redone into perfect curves. I smiled at her and she approached. We asked for more drinks, offering her one, too.

'You are beautiful – are you available for all night and are you OK being with me and him?' I asked her, and she nodded.

We paid the club bar bill and took the lady to the hotel. Mr Handsome was very excited. He was feeling free, not worried about people seeing him.

At the hotel, she walked straight into the reception. She already knew the rules. She needed to show her ID and they took a copy. Then we went straight to the room, where she started to take off her clothes. I just looked at her, thinking how strange the situation was. Her cock must be very tiny, I thought, and then I spotted her beautiful pussy. Mr Handsome looked at me and started to laugh.

'I think you chose the only girl in that club who doesn't have a cock,' he said and guffawed.

I looked at her and, before I could say anything, she told me, 'I am not a ladyboy. I am a woman.'

I said clumsily, 'Don't worry. You are stunning. What would you like to have a drink?'

It was a good night anyway. She left around four in the morning and we were so drunk and happy.

We definitely wanted to have a ladyboy after that though.

We went to another club and we got two. Mr Handsome looked at me and said, 'Just in case.' We went back to the hotel room. Mr Handsome was busy with one of them and I looked at the other and smiled.

She told me, 'I don't suck women.'

'Can I suck you?' I replied, already tipsy.

'Yes. You suck me.' So, I tried to suck her, but she was very soft. I asked her, 'How we are going to play? You don't suck women and your cock is soft.'

She shook her soft penis and said, 'Ladyboy don't like women. Look, is too soft.'

So, I said, 'But ladyboy likes my money. You told me you are bisexual. I paid six thousand baht for you both.'

'So?'

Mr Handsome was enjoying the other girl, so I smiled and gave up. 'So? OK, let's fucking get more drinks and watch them.'

That was our week, with no ladyboy for me, but we had some fun. Every day, there was swimming on the beach or in the pool and nightclubs and sex. We booked a boat to take us to an island, but Mr Handsome doesn't like the sun, so he stayed under a parasol, drinking and reading, while Mrs Kinky and the Fireman and I went swimming.

We started to chat. Mrs Kinky asked the Fireman to go for more drinks and then she started a different conversation with me.

'My husband is not a jealous man. We have money and he has his cup of tea. You need to learn to give him what he needs and he will look after you. Just remember, I am the most expensive whore he has ever had and that is how it must always be. We like you.' She smiled.

I was staring at her, speechless, admiring how strong and direct this woman was. I was embarrassed, though, and glad when our drinks arrived. It was my birthday and she had booked a dinner on the top floor of the Hilton Hotel. I couldn't have had it any better. It was a skyscraper and we had the best view in all of Pattaya. There were no 'ladies' that night. We decided to have a quiet night at the hotel with more drinks. They were spoiling me so much.

On the flight back, again in first class, I lay on the seat converted into a bed, having my last flutes of champagne, feeling amazed at how nice a life with money is. How my life had changed, how I had had so much luck since I left Peckham, and I was enjoying all of it.

At the airport, everybody said goodbye. A driver was waiting to for them and there was a cab to take me home, feeling happy and dying to hug my daughter.

I was still celebrating my birthday – I had booked a trip to Ibiza with two friends for a girls' party time.

The night before, I had a booking and it went on late because we were drinking wine. In the morning, my phone rang. 'You are late!' my friend screamed down the line. I ended up leaving my flat in a rush without tidying anything.

In Ibiza, the party started. On the first night, we went to a big club where a guy crossed over to me and gave me a hug, saying, 'Cute girl.' He held me in both arms and then disappeared. How annoying are these types of guys when they try to kiss or get hold of you? I took my bag and searched for my phone to make some videos, but I couldn't find it. It was gone. The guy had taken my phone from my bag. So many people were inside the club and they had disappeared in a second. It was pity, but it didn't disturb our fun, with drinking, beaches and an overall good time. I hadn't seen these friends for a while, and they don't know what I do for a living.

We got back to London and when I arrived at my flat, my key fob was not working. The concierge opened the door for me and told me to contact management.

I called the manager and asked, 'Why did you disconnect my fob?'

He said, 'You are doing business in your flat.'

'What are you talking about?' I said. 'I am not doing any business. Can you come here to talk to me, please?'

'I am busy now. I can't.'

I felt very nervous, but I had to keep going. 'You disconnected my access to my flat, accuse me of doing business there and now you are too busy? I am sure you have five minutes.'

'OK, give me ten minutes,' he said.

He knocked at my door and I was so anxious as I let him in. He stood by the entrance in front of my kitchen, where I was washing my dishes and doing some laundry.

'How come you accused me of doing business in my flat? What happened? Why did you come into my flat?'

'I got a report that there was a water leak in your flat. I tried to contact you, but your phone was off. So, I came in and saw all your toys around, plus you have a massage room. I went to your bedroom and saw more toys. What do you want me to think?'

I start to explain things to him. 'The massage table is for treatment due a scooter accident and I have problems with my back, so, once a week, I have a private physiotherapist who comes to massage me. And the toys are there because my boyfriend, who is the guarantor here, and I had a sex party before we went to Ibiza. Do I need to give you details about my personal life?'

(The massage room was for my clients for erotic massages, so I'm not sure if I convinced him.)

'No, you don't,' he said. 'But I won't give you access to the building.'

'I live here and have a contract and all my bills come here. Is that legal?' I asked him. 'Where is the water leak, by the way?' I added.

'We didn't find any.'

'Wait, so you came in and there was no water leak? You deny me access to my home with no letter based on what you have seen inside here?' I continued. 'Look, my boyfriend is my guarantor on this flat. He will want to talk to you. I am not doing any business here and if you want me to go, don't disconnect my fob, just talk to me and I will go. But he will be angry and if you cancel my lease, you will be hearing from him. You know who he is. You came into my flat, went inside my bedroom, which is my private room and does not have any water pipes. Isn't that an invasion of privacy? What are we gonna do?'

He looked at me and realised that he had made a mistake.

'OK, this is not a big deal. I made an error. Just be careful, please.'

He left and I exploded in tears. I was so scared. How horrible it is when we feel we're a shit, a nobody. It was lucky that he was a good guy and obviously saw that he could also be in trouble. This was my residence. By law, what I do is not considered a business, but I wasn't sure if that would protect me.

I called Mr Handsome, who never gets nervous, and he calmed me down. Of course he didn't care, as he has people who can solve any problem for him. He just pays for solutions. 'Don't be silly. He won't do anything, and if he asks you to move, we will rent another flat.'

For Mr Handsome, everything was so simple. He had answers for everything, but I was still nervous, so he asked someone who could give me legal advice to call me.

'You need to get rid of your friend. Don't let her meet any clients at your flat. Only you, because if you get a warning, you can be charged with subletting a room or running a brothel.'

How ridiculous it all is. I didn't get any money from Susy. She was just a good friend who sometimes used my flat, but he told me to stop.

I left my washing machine on and finally managed to sleep. In the morning, I went to make myself a coffee and saw water all over the floor. Oh my God, I really did have a water leak. By the time the manager came into my flat the water from the machine must have dried up and that was why they couldn't find anything.

Tony, the Australian client, used to text me constantly. It was against my rules, but he was single, and nice, so I made an exception. I needed to vent my frustration, so I called him and he said he'd come to have a look. Luckily, it was only a broken pipe and was easy to fix.

'You saved my arse, instead of taking it,' I joked to him, still feeling very nervous. He hugged me and stroked my face.

'You have enough people who use you. I don't want to be another one.'

I kissed him.

We went to the living room and chilled on the sofa. I rested my head on his lap while he stroked my hair. I asked him, 'What word would you use when you think of me?'

'Naughty,' he said, smiling, pulling my hair slowly. How I loved it.

'What about you, when you think of me? If you do?' he asked me.

I said, 'Peace; your messages make me feel less alone.'

We stayed there on the sofa for a long time. It had been a while since I'd felt that good.

He left my flat very late, as he worked shifts and needed to go to work.

29

There was a swinger's club near Heathrow where Mr Handsome loved to go. He booked a hotel room for us at the airport, so it was easy for me to get there on the Underground.

That night, they had some guys doing BDSM and this man tied a girl on a St Andrew's cross and started to whip her. I thought it was so sexy, but his hands weren't firm. I commented to Mr Handsome, 'He should do it a bit harder and be firmer.'

'I completely agree. So, you like that?' a black lady next to me asked, after hearing our conversation.

'Oh, yes, I do,' I replied, smiling and turning to look at her.

She turned her eyes on me. 'Should we go to the other room where there's the spider web and I can tie you up?'

I looked at Mr Handsome. He giggled and agreed with a smile.

We went to the room with the spider web made of rope, and, once I was stuck in the nest, she started to beat me with her hands. 'Not on my face,' I asked her, as I hate to be beaten there, so she only did it on my back. Her hand was firm.

'Let's see how horny you are,' she said, talking dirty. Then her husband came up behind me and fucked me right there. I was into the game and got to the stage of thinking only about my pleasure. I no longer saw anyone around me. It was just me and her hands. I wanted it harder and harder. My face was to the wall, so I did not realise that people were watching us. I only realised when we finished and I put my clothes on to leave the room, feeling bit embarrassed.

Mr Handsome was amazed. 'Good girl,' he told me.

'Oh, I forgot to say thanks to the couple,' I said, turning back, but she was on her knees, sucking her husband. He didn't cum, so I also got on my knees and she shared her lolly. He exploded. Well-deserved.

It was almost 2:00 a.m. and the club was about to close. We were sitting with another couple. The gentleman was an Asian businessman and he was talking with Mr Handsome, telling him about their experiences abroad in other famous places for swingers.

'I loved watching you tied to the nest,' he said, smiling, offering us a lift to the hotel so we could have more fun there, as the club was about to close. We ended up at the hotel and they bought some drinks. My drink had some drugs in it that I didn't know about, which made me feel a bit paranoid, and the end of the night was very confusing. Mr Handsome asked the others to leave as I was sick.

A few hours later, it was morning and I wanted to go home, so I got a cab and left the hotel.

At my flat, I was still in a panic. I felt so sick and couldn't sleep all day. I texted the Bite Man, as I hadn't seen him for a while. I almost felt like he had been avoiding me, as he had been ignoring my messages. But this time, he replied. 'They definitely put something in your drink. Drink plenty of water, put the TV on and watch a cartoon. Keep your brain busy.'

I spent all weekend in my bedroom. I missed Bite Man, but he did not say anything about seeing me.

Mr Handsome wanted to explore his fetish of watching other people fuck me. We stayed at St. Pancras, as it was easy to catch a train from there to visit another club, and this was one was outside London.

The place wasn't nice, though, and neither were the people. We didn't like the venue, but we decided to have a drink, since we'd come all the way there. We were not enjoying the place and I hadn't felt like going out that night, anyway.

A foreign guy came to talk to me. He smelt funny, so I looked at him and asked, 'Do you want me to fuck you?'

'Oh, yes. Of course. Should we go?'

'Are you sure you want me to fuck you?' I said and he nodded.

'Just to be clear and avoid misunderstandings – as I said, I wanna fuck you. My dildo is inside my bag and it is eight inches long. I want to stick it inside your bum. If you want, we can go.'

He ran away, calling me crazy, and we laughed about it all night.

'You are an ugly girl. Let's go to the hotel, I've had enough,' Mr Handsome said to me.

I still hadn't heard from the Bite Man. I sent him a few texts, which he read, but there was no reply. I hate it when people do that. I am not good at those games, making people wait, being a drama queen, being difficult, causing provocations or being indirect.

I liked him more than I should, and it was causing me a lot of frustration.

Doing what I do obviously gives me a chance to meet people, and some I can even risk asking out, if I want – like, Tony, the Australian guy who worked at the hospital, who fixed my washing machine. We had become quite close, but mostly just texted. Almost every day he would send me nice messages, so I agreed to go for a coffee with him.

He was so sweet. He listened to everything I said.

'Oh my God, your life is so busy and mine is so boring,' he replied.

We should go for more coffees, I thought, when he left me at my flat. I was intrigued that he did not try to have sex with me, but I felt embarrassed to ask him about it, so once he had left, I sent him a text:

Don't you like me?

I can't afford you.

What if I don't charge you?

We play in a different league.

It was a strange feeling to have someone who was not seeing me for sex. Many of my clients are so nice and friendly, but, obviously, sex is what it is all leading to. No one is really interested in being only my friend if sex is not involved, as that is what they want. Tony was not interested in the same things.

We started to chat more regularly. Every day, at any time of the day. Any small problem at my flat, he offered to help, as he was always very handy and available. I became used to calling him every day just to not feel alone. His voice was so calm, so peaceful. He made me feel so good and special.

Sometimes, I felt that I was getting too old to keep doing this work, and it crossed my mind to stop, even though I was still enjoying it. It didn't help that people kept posting a lot of feedback and field reports about me on that nasty forum.

Being popular also creates lots of expectations. Sometimes, they can be too much. I was very busy at that time with long bookings, and had very good clients – kinky men wearing expensive suits and ties, and I was their human fountain.

I completely forgot about the place where I had started. I was mostly acting like a sex machine and didn't realise that my body was starting to get tired. I don't take drugs, but there was lots of drinking and trying to not think of my Bite Man.

Tony texted me, saying he was at a hospital not too far away and inviting me for a drink. We spent the evening laughing and talking of silly things. My work, his work, life. He was becoming my best friend. His simplicity made me love to be around him. I had found someone who didn't see me just for sex.

Mr Adan, the diplomat, had been sending me lots of messages and pictures from the places where he went for work. That week, he had been travelling a lot. Sydney, Cape Town, Vienna, Budapest ... He had been quite romantic, too. I had the feeling he was trying to woo me. He was a such an educated and pleasant person, and it was flattering to have a man in his position interested in me.

He came to London often for business.

This particular time, he had spent all morning in a meeting at Whitehall and came after that to spend the afternoon with me. His flight was around 7:00 p.m., so he had plenty of time, but he decided to leave a bit earlier, as he had some work to do and wanted to get to the airport early to spend a little time on his laptop.

After he left, I laid on bed to rest and then I got a message from Mr Handsome.

Are you OK?

Yes.

But then I realised he never texted to just ask if I was all right. So, I replied, *Why?*

And he said, *Where are you?*

At my flat.

Didn't you hear the news? Westminster Bridge has just had a terrorist attack. Everything is blocked and you tell me you are at the flat? Get out right now.

Oh my God, so, that was why I had heard lots of sirens; I was used to ignoring them. I put my clothes on and went downstairs. I came across a huge commotion, with police everywhere and helicopters flying over Westminster Bridge. Television networks were everywhere with cameras and reporters. Chaos. Everything was blocked off; no one could pass through the police tape. I took a picture and sent it to Mr Handsome. He replied: *Get out of there. Go to your daughter's house.*

I put some clothes in a bag and took my car keys, but there was no way I could get out of the parking garage. I put my car back in its bay, walked out of the building to the first bus stop and left London for my daughter's house.

On the bus, I realised that Mr Adan had been out there. I was worried about him, so I sent him a text:

How are you? Are you safe? Did you hear about the attack?

I just got to the airport. I am in the BA lounge and just watching the news. I passed the bridge few minutes before that. London is getting crazy, stay safe.

I was relieved we were all safe. I spent a week out of London before going back to my flat.

30

I had a two-hour outcall booking. It was in a very posh, small and discreet hotel in Finsbury Square.

It was lunch time, so I arrived a bit early and texted the client. He said he was out. I sat at the bar and asked for a drink.

He arrived, smiling. 'Give me a minute, I still need to check in.' He went to see the concierge. After that, he came to the bar, asked the barman to put the bill on his room, and we went upstairs.

'You don't have any luggage?' I asked him.

'No. I am not staying here. This is just for the meeting.'

I stared at him, feeling flattered, looking at this very polite guy with a foreign accent, a handsome and well-dressed man.

We got to the room and started to chat. I asked him, 'What kind of service are you interested in?'

'Just talking.'

'What? You paid for an expensive hotel only to talk? And for two hours?'

'Yes, I did,' he said and smiled.

'Where are you from? What are we going to talk about?' I asked.

'Holland. And I speak your mother tongue, so it will be easier. I am married and love my wife. That is what we are going to talk about – we have two beautiful kids and recently I found out she is having an affair. She is going out with someone who hurts her. Sometimes, she arrives home and she has so many bruises. At the beginning, we had lots of discussions that went nowhere, but now I have decided to try to understand why she does it. She says that she can't help it. She just needs it and I shouldn't stop her going. I want my wife back, so, if it is so important to her, and she likes pain, I could do that to her, instead of someone else.'

I interrupted him. 'No, it doesn't work like that. Was she abused when she was a child?'

'Yes. But I won't tell you how.'

'That's fine. But you can't beat her.'

'Why not? Someone else does.'

'Because she loves you; you are the father of her kids; you mean happiness to her and the other person ... she probably has no feeling for him; she just uses him to punish her.'

'So, what should I do?'

'Just keeping loving her. Be patient, don't try to be the other guy. It doesn't work like that. She needs to find her peace of mind and stop blaming herself for whatever happened in her past.'

'On your profile, it seems like you enjoy so much play, including anal and domination games. If my wife blames herself, what about you? Do you have any blame in your life, or do you just do this for money, or to play with people who are victims of abuse? Why did you choose these services? Tell me about you.

I was not expecting this question, so I went quiet and got a bit nervous. But, when he looked into my eyes, hoping for an answer, he seemed genuine, so I started to talk about the guy with whom I first had anal sex. Hearing about his wife's frustration brought back memories of my own, and I found I wanted to share them.

'I lost my virginity to a guy who was much older than me He was a friend, but he wasn't the love of my life. I met someone a year later, who was also fifteen years older, and who made me completely lose my mind.

'I was very young and he was very ambitious and handsome. He was naughty and hard-working. Girls were always drawn to him. He had a good job, a good car and a good apartment. And me? I was a shy girl, still in school. I think he was probably the only person in all my life who I really loved enough to die for.

'It was Saturday night and he was trying to let me down by not answering my calls. I knew there was a party going in my town and he would be there. So, I went, and I saw him, and he wasn't alone. There was another young girl holding his hand, and I just went crazy.

'I approached him and we started to argue in front of everybody. He grabbed my arm and we left the club and went straight to his car. He was so angry. He drove me to a very quiet road and we kept arguing. Suddenly, he just ripped my clothes off, turned me over doggie style and, without any preparation, cleaning or lube, I had my first anal intercourse. I still remember how painful it was, but with my fear of losing him, the only thing I wanted was to see that man desiring me, so that made me have an orgasm despite the pain. That is probably the reason for all of this now.

'I never had any chance to win that man. Even months later, he never changed. One day, I was waiting for him in front of his building. His car approached and he had another woman with him. I had a bottle of ninety percent proof alcohol in my hand. I walked up to his car and poured it over her, showing her the match in my hand and saying, "Next time, I will light it." She started to panic and he tried to calm me down, as he knew how to deal with me. But the day after, when no one was in danger, he got so angry at me. This time, he had plenty of reason.

'I was so down and the relationship was toxic. He was affecting my life and, a few months after that, I got pregnant. I swear on my own life, it didn't happen on purpose.

'I was with him, feeling sick, and he gave me a tablet saying it was going to make me feel better.

'I lost my baby in pain on his toilet. I still have the imaged burned into my memories, of it coming out of me as I was screaming and how he came in and just flushed it away – that's what made my brain collapse. After sleeping for hours, I woke up and went to the kitchen to have some water and try to eat something. When I went to throw away the food I couldn't eat, I found a package in the bin of this strong medicine for cancer treatment, but which also causes abortions.

'My mum comes from a very religious family and she knew what was happening, as she is a mother and could tell I was suffering in silence. But she respected my pain and silence. I couldn't even look her in the face, I was feeling so ashamed.

'So, I decided to go abroad for a year to try to heal my pain and have a break with my dad, who was living abroad, but I didn't go back. It is now twenty-five years that I have lived abroad. I have tried to go back and live in my country a few times in the past, hoping that I might meet this man, look in his eyes and feel I was ready to forget about it. But I have never had that feeling. I was never ready to forgive, and I never forgot. Even years afterward, my legs would tremble and my voice stutter when I saw him. I knew it was a sign that I wasn't ready to live in the same place as him again.

'After many years, he came to London to visit me and we spent a weekend together, but with no sex. I wasn't the only one who had some issues to clear up with him. He said he wanted to apologise and see how I was. He also said that he hadn't forgiven himself. After more than twenty-five years, we had an intense hug and I told him that my anger was mainly with myself, because I had spent all this time wondering why I fell for a lover who was a monster. He said, "I am not a monster. I was just too scared and selfish."

'He looked at me and said, "I have done many things in life I regret. But not having that baby, and how I did it, is the biggest one. I know that it is hard to erase the past, and we can't go back, but I need to know you are OK."

'He was very honest. He had travelled all that way to say that and I could finally see true feeling in his eyes. I felt at peace.

'He left and I sat in the airport with tears on my face. My heart was hurting and I could not hold it all in, so I texted someone who bites me and gives me physical pain, like your wife does. This person punishes me by biting me very hard, leaving bruises, when I feel disquieted.

I was desperate to meet him. I told him: 'Come to see me if you are hungry.' He gets horny when I provoke him. He came to see me that night and he was starving. He said, 'You are the only person who lets me do what I do and really enjoys it.'

I just replied, 'I need to be punished.'

'Then, seven years ago, I had a boyfriend after my divorce, but he died in a motorbike accident. He was the second man who I loved. I never thought I would feel in crazy love again.

'We had a big argument and I wasn't talking to him, not even answering his phone calls.

'One night, he was drunk and he wanted to talk to me, so he got on his motorbike and, on his way to my house, crashed his bike and broke his spine.

'He was gone and I couldn't say goodbye. I couldn't tell him that I wasn't angry anymore; I had just wanted to punish him, but we were gonna be OK.

'It was too late. I was depressed for many years after that, thinking it was my fault. I should have answered his calls.

'When I started working as an escort, I found relief when I was tying people up and giving them a bit of pain, until I met the Bite Man. The stronger his bites, the harder he gets. He used to leave my body almost bleeding. I got addicted to him. I needed him to keep hurting me every time I was feeling guilt, sadness, or that I was alone.

'He never called me by my name and it makes me feel terrible. I have an obsessive desperation to see him but he always disappears, and, when I text him, he reads it, but does not reply because he is not interested in having any kind of relationship.

One day, I was sitting at a bar drinking with my best client, who had also become a friend, Mr Handsome. He noticed all my bruises and my sadness.

'He said to me, 'I think you should tell me more about these bites. He is not only a client, is he?'

'I told him about my feelings and he made me realise that it wasn't good for me. He advised me to start therapy, which would help me to stop to feeling guilty. His first advice was to not see the Bite Man at all, as a client or privately. The therapy did help me a bit, but she was not right about how my guilt worked.

'I thought that I needed to get treatment to not feel guilty anymore, to realise that nothing was my fault, but what really made a difference was not blaming the other side, to truly forgive those who hurt me. Now, when I go to my hometown, I see this man and I can have a good conversation with him. Many times I don't even think about what happened. We are good friends. I couldn't love him again, even though different eyes, but I can hug him with my heart and be his friend and feel at peace. My voice and my body don't tremble anymore. I have healed my wounds.

'I lost my other boyfriend as he chose to take a motorbike out when he was drunk. He killed himself. It is sad that he passed when I wasn't talking to him, but I did not kill him. Only true forgiveness heals the pain, and your wife has to do the same. She needs to find forgiveness to find peace.'

Do you think you can help her? I asked him.

He stared at me for a while, without saying a word, fixing his eyes on me. Then stood up. 'Thanks. Our meeting is finished.'

And we left the hotel.

31

H*ow frenetic is life here in London – everything happens so fast,* I was thinking as I walked under London Bridge station, listening to the loud noises of the train passing over the rails and watching the madness of numerous people passing by, rushing to work.

Most of the men who search for sex workers are not necessarily doing it because they are lonely or lack affection. We are in a different world here. Many people use sex as a way to de-stress and most come during the day, between breaks or during cancelled meetings. I am not a beautiful young girl, with a body to die for. My clients want my specific services or to try different things. I am talking about my real clients though, not the time-wasters.

When I open the door for a new client, it is a surprise for both parties. You don't know their face, their likes, their personality. As the years go by, we become calmer and feeler safer when we offer our services, but taking off your clothes in front of a stranger will always lead to a little nervousness and expectation. So, there's always some anxiety before opening the door, and I believe it is the same for the client, as they have no idea what they will find inside my flat.

This is the reason that many, when they have found their main requirements, such as safety, an affinity with the escort and satisfaction in the sexual act, will return, if they are the type of people who prefer to have a regular girl. Also, knowing who is behind the door makes a lot of difference when a sex worker is alone, without any support, in case of unwanted visits.

The moral judgment of society states that a married man is cheating and a pervert if he visits a sex worker and that is enough to cause the destruction of a family. Instead, the reality of a married man visiting a sex worker is simply about supplying a need he has perhaps lost over the course of a long life in a family, which creates a sense of guilt because his desire for a sex life continues.

Many define prostitutes as street walkers and escorts as people who receive clients in a private space. It doesn't matter what the definition is – my wish is that people would start to respect that society doesn't have reasonable standards.

Some people literally only get turned on by sex workers and, sometimes, they're even addicted to paying. But, mostly, paying is a good way to not feel guilty and not have any attachment or commitment towards a girl, especially when the client wears a ring on their left hand.

Society needs to defend and empathise with those who don't have choices, the people who are vulnerable, independent of what is right or wrong, and stop criticising only those who are socially undesirable, instead of following what is politically correct. I would never call myself a victim because of all the bad experiences in my past, as they didn't bring me to sex work.

Accusing and pointing fingers is so easy, but putting up a fight against the system is not. Fighting for our rights doesn't get any results if you don't change people's minds. If the way people think doesn't change, having rights will not make any difference.

People fight against racism, women fight for equal rights, gays fight to end homophobia and we carry on, arguing and, many times, resorting to aggression, but, if the other side doesn't change their views, we will never be equal and we will never get any real positive results; everything becomes worthless.

In fact, seeing people in better situations attracts attention, and envy and desire creates respect.

When you see people in inferior situations, you can feel sorry for them, but then a feeling of superiority follows, an involuntary feeling of satisfaction for being in a better situation.

Look at people doing hard work, like a guy cleaning the road or a waiter serving a table. You can be sure that the guy cleaning the road would prefer to be in an office, and the waiter would prefer to be sitting at the table themselves. I prefer to be in a hotel with a client than to be the cleaner of the room.

Whoever is in a better situation looks slightly behind them. I understand that someone must do all these jobs in life and often it's those who did not have a choice or the opportunity to be in a better position. It is the same when I talk about changing my work or stopping. My clients smile, but they are not really interested in seeing me doing it. On their side, they want me where I am because if I left I wouldn't be available anymore for their needs. I am making an uncomfortable situation comfortable for them.

Adan, the diplomat, offered to change my life. I got an email saying that was coming to London, that his wife had passed away and he needed to resolve things here and wondered if we could spend a weekend together.

It was shocking news, but I was flattered to be his choice in that delicate moment. I went to pick him up at the airport. I was expecting a lovely weekend where we'd go walking, but he seemed distressed about what had occurred. He booked dinner at OXO, where I wanted to try pigeon, and he made me an offer.

'I would like you to move to France, to my villa.'

I gasped. 'Why me?'

He said, 'Why not?'

'Don't you think it is too early for you to choose another woman?'

'No. I don't.'

'Can we let the weekend together pass and then I can decide?'

'Sure, my dear,' he answered. Smiling, he raised his wine glass and took a sip.

We had a good time, but, on the second day, we talked about how my life would be.

'With your influence, would you help me to find a job there? I don't even speak French.'

'You don't need to work. You will have a good life and I will not let you miss out on anything. You can join me on many trips and look after my villa. It'll be a completely new life for you.'

That night in bed, I was struggling to sleep, processing it all. He likes beautiful women; he travels a lot, and I kept imagining what my life would be like.

I left my husband because we were in a very boring marriage. OK, he had money and could take me on lots of trips, but that was not enough when considering living with a person for the rest of my life. It was difficult to believe, but I had found my sexuality in sex work and I enjoyed my lifestyle.

In the morning, I had my answer. 'If I leave everything here and go with you, one day, you meet another woman. I will lose everything and be old and with no money. I need a job.'

'I would never do that to you.'

'You did it to your wife and mother of your kids. She passed away and you already had thought of who was going to replace her, even before you buried her. I can't accept your offer.'

I should have chosen a better way to tell him, as he didn't like that. He left in the afternoon and never contacted me again.

I invited Tony to my flat. We had been friends for over two years, but with that level of attraction and interest, we couldn't stay just as friends. Desire was in the air. I cooked dinner and opened a bottle of wine. And, for first time of my life, I made a proposal to a man.

'Do you want to be my friend with benefits? I really like you and my therapist agreed with me that I need to start to hang out with more people.

I want to make new friends and see some normal people, especially if they're single and not in my line of business.'

'Can we go slowly?' he asked me.

He seemed a bit scared of me. We decided to start off as just good friends.

He would call me every day, just to say, 'Good morning.' We spent so many hours chatting when he had a break. We did lots of video calls and I was feeling much better as a person and less lonely. He enjoyed listening to my stories about my crazy clients, always calling me 'naughty girl.' We were very close. I could talk to him about everything. He didn't judge me.

Susy wanted to check the number of someone who had booked her, so she tried Facebook. She was still concerned about the knife on her neck incident.

'I didn't even know that we could do that,' I said to her, and I laughed. 'Let's try to find Tony.'

It wasn't difficult to find him on Facebook using his phone number. The pictures matched, but the name was wrong. We started to have a look at his profile and scrolled through his gallery – I got a shock when I saw a picture of his wedding and two children. He said he was single. It sounded weird, as we were just friends and he knew all my secrets, so why was he lying to me, even about his name?

I sent him a text:

Hey, how are you? What are you doing? Fancy a drink tonight?

Hi, I am still at work. Doing a double shift.

Why did you never tell me you are married and have two beautiful kids? Or even your real name?

I don't remember that part of my life. Lol.

I sent him a screenshot of his kids and his wedding.

In that case, you should be more careful when you set the privacy of your Facebook.

I will call you in ten minutes.

My phone rang. 'I am so sorry,' he said. 'I didn't want to lie to you.'

'So why did you?'

'Firstly, because when I met you and paid for your services, I felt guilty, but we had good sex and a good chat. I liked you and now we are friends and I thought it was too late. I am falling for you and I know we have different lives. I still live with my wife, but we are not together anymore. We are just good friends and we are waiting for a good time to separate. My son is still too young and we think it is better to wait a bit more. We still have a good friendship. She doesn't mind that I go out or stay out. She does that as well.'

'I still don't see a reason why you didn't tell me.'

'Yes, it was silly. I am very sorry. My feelings for you are getting strong. You see so many clients with money who are well-educated. I feel so frustrated. I wish you had a different life. A bit more normal.

'Can we meet tomorrow?' he asked me. 'Let's go for a drink.'

I met him the next day and he was standing waiting for me near the bar. Tony was a calm person, never raising his voice and never getting angry. It was so peaceful when he talked and his arms were very warm and cosy when he hugged me; he was very protective. He explained everything and gave me a big kiss. I was relieved. We slept together that night. He held me all night and I felt so protected. I hate people touching me when I am sleeping, apart from my daughter. But that night was different. I just wanted to the warmth and smell of his body.

It was Friday and time again to meet the crew at the hotel. Mrs Kinky had gone to the theatre with the Fireman, so it was only me and Mr Handsome, laughing and chatting in the bar. I told him about what happened with Adan, but didn't feel ready to talk about Tony.

He asked me, 'Do you regret turning down this opportunity?'

'Not really. But it could have been a chance for me to have a different life.'

He laughed, shaking his head. 'You don't need a man to change your life or to make you stop. You can change your life whenever you want. When he made you the offer, what was the first thing what came into your mind?'

'I felt sorry to think of losing my flat, my life, my clients, and to enter a boring life with someone who I don't even love.' Then I thought of Tony, but didn't mention that.

He giggled. 'There you are. You already know what you want.'

I stood and walked to the toilet then, wearing my seamed stockings as always. It was incredible how he enjoyed them.

While I walked to the loo, I saw someone familiar. He smiled and I kept walking. On the way back, he stopped me. 'Hey, Lily, do you remember me?'

'Oh, yes, of course. You are an Italian banker who came to see me a few times.'

'That's right; are you working tonight?' he asked.

'I am with someone,' I said. 'But you can join us for a drink, and perhaps in bed, as we have a room here, if you fancy. He won't mind.' And I walked away, smiling.

Back with Mr Handsome, I told him, 'There is someone here who I know.'

He laughed. 'Why you didn't invite him to join us?'

I gave him a naughty look and said, 'I did.' We giggled. Five minutes later, he approached us.

We chatted for a while and had more drinks. Then Mr Handsome invited him to the room.

We went to the room and right away started to take our clothes off. Mr Handsome sat on the sofa. He loved watching. The Italian guy was very horny and started to eat my pussy and, after that, it was my turn to suck him. We fucked, he came quickly and when we finished, he went to shower and then it was Mr Handsome's turn. He loved it.

32

We spend our lives searching for happiness, often wondering if it actually exists, as we never feel completely happy; this is just part of humankind. All we can do is try to make happy moments, and, in my opinion, we need three elements to do this: money, sex and love.

There is a lot of disagreement about this, as some think health is the most important thing – for me, health is a priority in life, but it is not what builds happiness. We usually only consider our health when we feel the risk of losing it. In practice, health is just a part of life, and we don't think about it when we're stressed or working too much. Also, if it is so important, why do people smoke, drink and eat junk food?

At the end of the day, we think of other things before worrying about our health. Most of the time, we only change our habits for the better when something bad happens. I had this same conversation when I met Toby.

Toby was paraplegic. He sent me an email asking me to visit him at his house, but it had to be at 2:00 a.m. because his mum was going to be asleep next door. His carer would get him ready and switch off his emergency button, so we could have a bit of privacy.

I arrived and had to hold back my tears. I was saying, 'Oh my God, I don't know if I can do this,' as my legs were trembling. I entered his room and stood there for a few seconds, frozen. He was so young, angelic and handsome, with an impressive smile. He was lying on his bed, his hair combed with gel and wearing a subtle cologne.

'Hey, Toby, nice to meet you,' I said, approaching his bed and trying to start a chat. This time, I was the one who was nervous and needing a strong drink.

He led the conversation. 'Is this your first time seeing a disabled person?'

'No. I have had some clients in a wheelchair, but it is my first time with someone paraplegic. Which parts of your body you can feel?'

'Only from my neck up to my head. I feel my arms, but not below my elbow. I have strong pain in my neck.'

I held his cheeks with my hands and started to caress him, giving him a kiss. He closed his eyes, saying, 'It is so good, don't stop.'

'Sit on my face; I want to taste and smell a woman.'

'Do you feel anything down in your genitals? I mean, do you get hard?'

'Only tingling. I would do anything to feel hard again. But it has never happened since the accident.'

I finished my hour and asked him, 'Can I lie down beside you for a bit?'

'Yes, sure.'

'Do you mind if I touch your genitals?'

'No other girls have asked me that. Are you sure you want to do it?'

'Yes, I am.' I removed his blanket; his legs were so thin, already atrophied by the years. I couldn't keep going, so I lay down beside him and kept caressing him. It was too emotional for me.

'What happened to you?'

'I had an accident on a scooter seventeen years ago. I was nineteen. I broke my spine.'

'I lost a boyfriend in a motorbike accident. He also broke his spine but didn't make it. Do you think he would have preferred to live or die? How do you feel about being alive?'

'When it happened to me, for so many years, I wished I'd died. I spent a long time so upset, but now, I have learnt to accept it. I survived and I live for my mum.'

We kept chatting for another hour and I asked him, 'If you could choose to walk again or feel horny, what would you choose?'

Without any hesitation, he said, 'I have gotten used to not walking, but I never accepted not having sex. I was young and always horny when I could feel things, so I would choose sex. That is why I keep booking girls. It is late and I need to take my medicine. Would you see me again?'

'Yes, of course.'

I stood and dressed myself and was about to leave when he said, 'Thanks for tonight. Your envelope is beside the TV.'

When I turned back, I kissed his lips, saying, 'Merry Christmas, my dear, you gave me a gift today. I can't take your money. I will meet you once a month, if you want, but I can't take any money from you.'

Toby was the only client who I never charged. We met many times and it was so lovely to see his face, shining, energetic and intelligent.

He spent most of his time watching TV or on his computer, and, by using his chin, he wrote, surfed on internet and saw the world from inside his apartment, which was all adapted for him. When I met him, we kissed, I cuddled him, massaged his neck. I sat on his face and massaged his penis with oil and he got erect, but never hard.

Then he did not contact me for a while. I was worried that something had happened to him. I was not allowed to contact his mother. But, one day, I got a message and we met up again. He was tired, but alive.

The day after my first meeting with Toby, Susy came to work with me at my flat. We had a few bookings and I let her use my spare bedroom. It wasn't busy and, after the bookings, we started to have a few drinks and chat. It had been a while, so we started to update each other on our gossip.

'I went to an outcall last night. He is paraplegic and had the same accident as my ex-boyfriend.'

Susy said, 'I couldn't do that. For me, it would be too much to see someone in that situation and take their money.'

'I didn't charge him. I promised to see him once a month without charging.'

'You crazy? Now you want to be Madre Teresa?'

Laughing, looking at my bills and counting things up, while taking sips of wine, I said to her, 'Oh, dear, I've got to pay rent, pay bills, pay this and that, and we never have enough. At the end, we never have much money left.'

She smiled sarcastically and said, 'Of course, you can't make money if you don't charge. You have pleasure with your clients; you consume too much of your energy. You should be like me, just hold it all in and don't cum.'

We were already tipsy, so I said, 'How can you do that? Don't you feel frustrated when you can't orgasm with your clients?'

'I just hold it in and, after, if I am really horny, I just take my toy and finish myself off at the end of the day.' We both laughed.

But that was an actual joke, because Susy had met a client who she liked and I suspected that she was falling for him. It was her birthday, so they went out for dinner and then she called me, telling me that they were going to a strip club and, after, she would like to have a foursome, suggesting I invite Tony. I texted him, as he had never had one. He was very excited to come and join us.

Susy and her client arrived. She was tipsy and Tony was feeling a bit shy, but, after few more drinks, he relaxed and *voilà*, all our clothes fell off.

When we swapped partners, though, I felt jealous watching him fucking my best friend. I was furious. I started to drink more and stopped playing with Susy's client, who was also jealous over her.

He said, 'I am falling in love with her and I have enough money. I want to take her out of this life.'

'Don't play the saviour. You know she has two kids? Do you know she is married? Are you? Would you really take a sex worker with two kids into your life? It is not a joke and it is not funny.'

I was very irritated by seeing Tony with Susy. I felt my face burning and I was annoyed about everything, I felt as if I was losing control. I don't usually feel jealousy about any man, but I was relieved when Susy and her client left. Tony came to me and tried to hold my hand, but I pushed him away. 'I am jealous about you,' I said. And then I passed out.

I woke up in the morning and he wasn't there. There was a glass of water on my beside table. I picked up my phone and there was a message from him saying, *I love you.*

I couldn't think. I held my forehead, whispering, 'SHIT.' I drank the whole glass of water and lay down again in bed. I didn't want to think about anything.

He realised I had read the message and called me. 'Good morning.'

'I thought you might be upset with me,' I replied.

He was so sweet and calm. 'I would never be upset with you. I love you.'

After the call, I spent all day in bed, with the blackout curtains down, leaving my room in complete darkness. I started to recall the years since I started escorting, thinking of all the different kinds of men who had come into my life. The truth was, Tony was too ordinary to me. He was so normal, but he had become the person who was there when I wanted to talk, and I would call him if I wanted to cry, if I wanted a hug. He had the power to make me forget the world, the power to make my bad day become a great day. I felt lonely that day. I don't have anyone to go to bed with or get a hug from and I don't hear the words 'Good night' Tony was the one who was doing all that.

33

Mr Handsome was back from his family holidays. They had spent almost two months away, so we arranged a reunion.

I was not in the mood for crazy things. I had been feeling lonely and a bit too sentimental.

'My life is about cocks; everywhere I turn, I see cocks, I suck cocks and I fuck cocks,' I said to him.

'How lucky you are,' he joked, understanding that I was not in a good mood.

'It is probably time to have a break and do something different. Would you help me to open a new business to earn in a different way? I am tired of always lying to all my friends and family (except my sister, who knows but doesn't agree with my choice to do this). Always lying about my living and feeling that I am doing something wrong.'

He replied and, as always, was very direct. 'This is what you do, and this is what you are good at. Nothing will earn you more than this.'

I felt a bit frustrated by this answer. I was feeling cold and tired. I don't offer a girlfriend experience, as my services are all about filthy fucking (I've been told that I am not a woman fit for any man). I think he was surprised by seeing me a bit disinterested in my job.

I left the hotel in the morning. Instead of taking a cab, I wanted to take the tube, to see people and walk a bit. I got a sushi takeaway and sat by the river to have my lunch. Southbank is so magic, but sadness mixed with loneliness was twisting my heart. Being free is so important in the life of an escort, without the headache of a relationship. The key to success is not to get too personal and just enjoy the company of your clients. There can be no jealousy, as no one belongs to anyone and there is no drama. It is all about fucking, pleasure and money. But here were all these feelings. Did I want my own man? All to myself? My life didn't permit it.

Jan is my client from Norway. I first met him when I was still in Kensington. Our chats had the power to make me feel better. His wise words gave me comfort. We went to dinner and he spent the evening with me.

Rarely do I work on weekends. Those are my rest days. On Sunday, the day dawned sunny, so I decided to go jogging; contemplating the Thames always gives me a glow. I started to observe people. Almost I never do that, as tourists are everywhere.

A boy was doing the trick of making things vanish underneath a cup. How can people still fall for that? A woman was taking pictures, pointing her finger at the London Eye, and a newly married couple were posing for photos in front of Big Ben. All of us were contemplating the wonder that is this city. I had it all, right here. I could never have dreamt I'd be here one day, and yet here I was. I live in the heart of London, in of one of most prestigious buildings in Southbank, but I had the feeling that it did not matter much to me anymore. I just felt like an insignificant person in the middle of a crowd. That is what we are. A number in this life.

I didn't want to take any bookings. I wanted to see Tony, but he cancelled at the last minute, saying that he was tired and had a bit of flu. I got very angry and said, 'I am tired of your lies. Why don't you tell me the truth? Just tell me, are you still married?' And I got no reply. So, I threw my glass of wine at the wall.

With sadness, I thought how I would miss his calm voice. But he was another one who was now gone.

I love walking along the Thames. I usually take the route from Vauxhall to Tower Bridge. I like to see people around the London Eye. There are two people who play music on the street there, the saxophone and the guitar. To me, these two people are magical. The sound of the sax gives me great inner peace. I could sit there and just listen to them for hours. The guitar singer brings me happiness, too. It's good to be there, reflecting. I realised that I had been too emotional and vulnerable.

Marc, the actor, came to see me around then. He lives in LA and was passing thought. I loved seeing him. I was needing cuddles, and we had a good conversation. We opened a bottle of prosecco and chatted all night. It lifted me up.

'I love to talk with you,' Marc said, 'but can you tell me what really turns you on? What do you want in life?'

'Being a sex worker turns me on, but I became a sex machine,' I replied, and he laughed.

People come to me only because of sex. They want to see me get wet, they want to try things that they don't do in their normal life. And, of course, I do really enjoy that, as, if I didn't feel pleasure, I could not do all this. But there comes a certain point when you close the door at the end of the day and you say to yourself, 'I'm tired.' You just want to have a normal night.

Often, I'm ashamed of what I do. Then, I think of people who do other things that I would never have the courage to do. Someone must do every role in life. I have so many men who come to visit me and they're mostly married, but only a few – I can count them on my fingers – have admitted that they don't love their wives anymore. Mostly, they just complain about a stale sex life and their wives letting them down in bed. Most just want to keep desiring their wives. In a stereotypical family, as time passes, women lose their appetites and men don't stop loving their partner, but the relationship has ended up feeling like sleeping with a stranger. Or, as with food, you can't eat the same thing every day. Occasionally, you need a restaurant.

Personally, I find it very selfish when the partner does not respect the other's needs or will. Usually, these are the men who end up paying a girl to have the sex, as they don't have it at home anymore. Then society says they need to feel guilty, just for satiating an instinct which we all have.

The same goes for the woman, who sacrifices her personal needs for the family and kids. How many women lose their self-esteem and have no time for themselves and their friends? Having a family shouldn't be that way, causing pain or sacrifice, and, again, I think about how the system and our mentality are so wrong. We are living in a world where we have a sex war: men versus women.

So, what is wrong with paying for sex? If you are married and you just stay for convenience, or for the money, is that wrong? If you feel frustrated at work or are just doing it because you need to pay your bills, is that wrong? At certain times, and for many reasons, we all prostitute ourselves, but only my type of work is the wrong type, apparently.

Sex workers don't destroy marriages. In fact, we offer stability to a stereotypical marriage. We keep the balance when the man must hold together the financial stability of the family and must face all the stresses and pressures of work. It is naïve or selfish to think that husbands can live without any relief, when in their marriage, they don't have any comfort.

When a married man makes the choice to pay for sex, it is a way to feel less guilty. It reminds me of my married life, and the many times I arrived home and saw my husband as my stability, but we completely lacked any connection sexually. If we had had affairs, I wonder if we would still be together, or if our relationship just had to end, as nothing lasts forever. When the relationship is worn out, the love transforms into convenience or feelings of pity.

It gets to the point that one will look at the other, and we are either staring up at them or looking down on them. We're never at the same level, and the one who feels inferior ends up being humiliated or begging for love. Love is not about begging, though. It must be felt and no one will love a person who they feel sorry for. Love has to happen naturally and we need to feel respect. I am not sure of what I need now, or if what I am looking for is love.

I ended my marriage feeling sorry for my husband. It is sad when you get to that point. I felt he was the love of my life, the one who I chose to spend my time with, but he became the last person in this world who I would sleep with. How tricky is the heart.

I hide how I make my living. I lie to my friends, as I don't come from a rich family and now I support my parents. I spoil my mum and pay for everything she wants. I've found a way to compensate her, buying her forgiveness for when she suffered, when I lost my child and left home feeling ashamed, but also for when she found out about my dad's affair and I knew about it. I am also playing the system. My dad thought I had a rich boyfriend in Mr Handsome. And he was proud of it, but if he knew what I did, he would not even look me in the face. What is the difference between being with a rich man just for his money and selling my body? It's just private or public sex work. I am not hurting anyone. And even if I was, in many circumstances of life we make mistakes and we get hurt, or we hurt someone else.

We are all different and no one is perfect. Thinking that everything you do is correct or perfect is very hypocritical, in terms of work or in your social or love life. In any situation, we can do the right thing or the wrong thing; everyone has the right to decide that for themselves, to fight for their own survival and to improve their quality of life. So, the fact that I lie to my family and my friends about how I make my living is the only thing that makes me sad.

Sometimes I wonder if I'm unhappy, but I don't think so. I love being with my clients; they give me the best lessons I could ever learn in life. Some people gave me bad times, but, mostly, because I chose this life, sex work gave me the opportunity to change my life in every aspect and made me a better person. But I don't want my daughter to be judged because of her mother.

When I started doing this, everything was so new to me. Of course, it was for money, but I met the naughty side of myself, too. Regaining my sexual life was a great thing, honestly. I had to learn to say yes, and no. I met so many new people and I saw myself rising above the sorts of people who I used to encounter. And I like it all. I enjoy spending my afternoons and even late hours drinking wine and chatting with intelligent people.

But in all of this, I forgot about my personal life, and my friends. I didn't see that time was passing and that the body also changes. I'm not a young lady anymore. Now I need to make more choices for my future. I don't want this time to be wasted, just waiting for the future. When it comes time for me to stop, I must make plans and create new projects, but, at the same time, I have to enjoy this moment because in the future, it will be gone. My clients will go back to their families; they will close their doors and stay together. I am paid for my service and then I close my door and I am alone. So, after a certain amount of time, you can't help but feel lonely. I felt jealous about not having a complete family.

I started questioning women like me, who men do not invite to eat a pizza at home, sitting on the sofa and watching TV. Or to go to the movies. Or to take a walk in the mall. Their main expectation is to end up in my bed. They remember me when they want to fuck. Even if they want it in a romantic way, to go for a drink and a chat, it is, ultimately, about fucking.

That night with Marc, he didn't bite me, he didn't slap me, he didn't make me gush. He doesn't expect much. He listened to me and I enjoyed it a lot, as he let me put everything out there. And that really lit me up. I ended up realising that the worth of sex is having what we don't have. We're looking for what we don't often do. And I think now, at this stage of my life, I've experienced almost everything. I need what I don't have: just normal sex. This is what will give me pleasure now.

I need something different and, for me, vanilla is different. (We had a great night.)

I would love to change the world's mentality, but I can't. I would be happy if I could at least make someone who is reading this reflect on their life and their own intimacy at home, and to make that better. The rules don't matter; family is precious and we only have one life.

34

My phone rang one day. It was Mrs Kinky on the phone. Very unusual. She never called me. I answered and my face went pale.

'Mr Handsome is in the hospital. He has heart problem and needs a bypass. I am abroad at the moment at our summer house, but have got a flight for tomorrow. Can you go to the hospital and stay with him?' she asked me.

I ran to the hospital and, truly, it touched me a lot. I was afraid I'd lose him. And not for his money. I was afraid of losing a friend. At times he had been the only friend I had and I didn't see him just as a client anymore. I was a little psychologically weak during this period. I was used to seeing him being very arrogant, in fancy places, wonderful hotels, all just laughs, enjoying the best of the best. Then, suddenly, the person's health goes and they're in a hospital and so weak. This was what I saw when I opened the door to his room.

We went for a walk downstairs and he said, 'No matter how much money I have, when we are in bed in a hospital, we are all the same. We're just a number. Money helps, and perhaps you can die with a certain comfort, but, in the face of the problem, we are all practically the same.'

Money buys almost everything, but it doesn't buy your life.

'One day, I am a big boss, an arrogant and important person, and the next, I'm in an intensive care bed, just a number, fighting to live. I felt how insignificant we all are. And it was shocking.'

I had no words. We believe that money doesn't buy happiness, but we need money, sex and love to be happy.

The nurse came to do a blood transfusion and he asked me to leave, as he knows I faint when I see blood. I didn't want to leave him, knowing how miserable he was feeling, but he looked at me and said, 'Go home.'

I left the hospital, jumped in a cab and burst into tears.

This was not a glorious time.

You abandoned me. I couldn't resist sending a message to Tony. I got a reply in less than ten minutes.

Haven't forgotten about you, don't be silly. What are you doing tomorrow? I have a flight to Australia. Wanna meet before it?

Yes, sure.

When I opened the door, he gave me a tight hug. 'I thought you were angry,' I whispered in his ear.

'Never! Let's go for some food, I'm hungry.'

'My mum is in the country. She had an operation and I've been very busy. I had to look after her. Tomorrow, I am going on a flight to Australia to take her back.' This is how he explained his absence while we were waiting for our food.

As always, he was gentle, calm and peaceful. We had a hilarious conversation about my job and how many things I had learned, but also about my bad days and how I manage to deal with all kinds of different people, the nasty people and the friendly, as well as the great and rich clients.

'I have not had many women in my life. All your experiences about sex sound so crazy that it makes me feel jealous. I would love to try more different things, but I am still too shy for that.'

We went back to my flat and had another bottle of prosecco and a nice, hot bubble bath. I lit the candles in my bathroom and my personal room and made the atmosphere very romantic. (I never mention or take any man into my private room with the bigger toilet and bath – clients only go into my playroom and use the guest bathroom. I never bring anyone in my personal bed as I keep it only for me.)

That night, all I wanted was to forget about the world. My work phone was switched off. He knew exactly where to go on my body and we were just enjoying the moment. I sat on top of him and he whispered 'It is so good' as he penetrated me, romantic music playing in the background.

The sex with Tony was amazing and peaceful. Did we make love? No, we didn't. But I felt that he studied me and my body just to give me perfect pleasure. We had a farewell night and he left me completely drained.

A few weeks later, he came back home and we started to see each other very often and in a different way – as love partners. It had been many years since I had someone like that in my life. Even though we were not living together, we were communicating all day, every day. We talked about ten times a day, even just to say hello, have a nice day, etc. I felt he fitted well into my life.

If I cooked, he helped me with anything I needed, if he was available. He was extremely protective. He was never angry. He was almost perfect, a man who any woman might dream of being with.

He had a day off and we said we would spend it together. We planned to have an easy and lazy day, enjoying the sauna and swimming pool in my building, cooking together and watching some movies. But at 6:00 a.m., I got this message:

Morning, love, friends surprised me last night and were at my house when I got in and we were drinking all night. I am really sorry I don't like to mess you around, but I am tired and still drunk. Sorry I really need sleep.

And I couldn't even take any bookings. So disappointing.

A couple of days went by, and I hadn't heard from him. I tried to call several times and he did not answer, so I sent a message. *Why don't you answer my calls?*

The chest tightness I felt while I was checking my phone, so anxious, lasted another day. Finally, he answered:

Hi love, I have been very busy at work and plus got a man flu which made my week horrible and stressful.

'There's something that's not right, but I can't figure out what. Everything was going so well,' I told Susy, as I needed to talk to someone.

'Of course, he is still with his wife. Don't be a fool,' Susy told me.

'But he didn't have any reason to lie to me. We have been friends for over two year,' I replied, then turned on her. 'What about you? How are things going with your rich saviour lover?'

She giggled. 'He rented a flat here in London and wants me to move in with him.'

'What? And you call me foolish? What about your family?'

'He moved to London and separated from his wife. I didn't ask him to do that, because I didn't intend to leave my family. Being just a mistress was fine, but he's got an attitude about it, and now he's pressing me to leave sex work and stand beside him.'

'Oh, dear, so things are serious. Did you make a decision?' I guessed her answer by looking at her expression I hugged her and gave her a kiss on the cheek.

She got quiet, and I insisted. 'Go on. Tell me the truth.'

'I already left my house. The atmosphere at home was very bad and I was worried it would affect the children. My husband is a good man and a good father. I left a week ago. We're working on settling things in a friendly way.'

I was stunned. 'Why didn't you tell me before?'

'You have been going through some drama, too. And I don't want any more confusion. It was a serious decision that I wanted to take by myself.'

'You know what? You are right. He decided to leave his wife, you decided to leave your family, and I don't have the right to judge you. Let's open some prosecco to celebrate your victory – or your beheading,' I said, hugging her, with my heart tight, so afraid for my friend.

Is there anything that you want to tell me? I am starting to think that your commitments are not only to your work. But I am not in the condition to demand any explanation.

I texted Tony, thinking that I might also have issues with my relationship.

I am going to see you soon.

That was the only answer he gave me, and it was a few more days before I heard anything. It was a surprise when I received a message:

I am sorry I haven't seen you. But work is busy and it is paying good money to be there right now. I can come to see you today after work.

Yes, today after 6p.m. is good, I said, without any argument, although I think that he could have had the time for at least one message. But I didn't want to upset him. I wanted him and I didn't want anyone else in my client list. I would never be the lover of a married man, as that would be crossing a line I never was interested in crossing. I want my own man and won't share with anyone. But how was I going to demand that, having this lifestyle? It was so frustrating for me, the feeling of not having the right to demand anything. I decided to give Tony a chance.

A few months passed, and then, suddenly, he started to be more controlling about my time with my clients and very jealous about my job. He wanted to know everything I was doing, thinking I might have another man who I liked. Of course, I do have many nice clients and my life is about sex, so I felt sorry for him. I chose him to bring into my personal life, and only him, but he was making me feel very guilty. 'There is only you in my private life,' I kept telling him.

I had to report every meeting I had to him, and how long it went on. Every day, he called me to say good morning, and told me how much he loved me before and after my meetings. I could no longer spend any extra time with my clients because he got jealous, accusing me of enjoying being with them, and I started to feel suffocated, so I took the decision to stop seeing him. I needed a break to think about things.

35

I ended up going to Berlin with my friend who was a Brazilian fighter and lived in America. I met him as a client, but we ended up being good friends.

We planned to arrive at the same time and met at the airport in Berlin. He was flying in from Italy and I arrived from London just twenty minutes after him. We got a cab to the hotel. He took me for a walk and to visit Checkpoint Charlie, then we went back to the hotel and got ready for a sex party.

The club was not busy. It had a round sofa in the middle of the dance floor. The rule was, if you lay on it, you got fucked. And that night there were so many hungry guys.

After a few drinks, I started to walk around the club. I love watching and it did not take long for me to feel ready to get going. But, also, I don't take long to get drunk either. I spotted this guy watching me. I sat at the bar and he came up. He looked at my feet and I looked at him, then I took my shoes off and showed him my bare feet, nails varnished on a dark red colour. I asked him, 'Do you like my toes?'

He held my feet, contemplating them, before starting to kiss and suck them.

'You are submissive, aren't you? I asked him.

'Yes, mistress,' he replied.

I laughed so loud, saying in high voice, 'Oh my God! Exactly what I need.'

I spotted a hook to hang someone on. Also, there was some rope, gloves, lube and condoms around. I sipped another glass of wine while he was enjoying my toes, and my friend approached, asking, 'Are you OK?'

I laughed. 'Don't worry. I am comfortable in my environment.'

I finished my glass of wine and asked my new friend, 'Should we try some BDSM?'

He giggled, saying, 'Oh, yes.'

'Come with me,' I said, and I stood, took his hand and walked to the stage where the hook and ropes were.

I wrapped his hands in the rope, threw it up over the hook, then grabbed the end, so he could hang from it.

The club stopped and people stood in a circle to watch us. I was very drunk, but I managed to do my little show. I lowered his pants and started stroking his body. Then, I put on a glove and, with the lube, start stroking his anus and sticking my fingers in.

'Do you like that?'

'Yes, mistress.'

I slapped his bum and continued, but the drink was already too much and I could not untie him. I called for help and some men came to sort it out.

Warning: When someone is hanging, a few minutes is OK. Any longer and it hurts and can cause injuries. Light BDSM is very sexy and fanciful, but it's not always a good idea to go too hard.

Some men started touching me then. One said to me, 'Now it's time for you to go to the sofa.'

I laughed, saying, 'Not yet,' and went to the bar.

I ordered another glass of wine and the waiter said, 'I think you need a glass of water.'

Six men came around me then. They were already desperate for me to go to the sofa in the middle of the room, but my head was clouded by drink.

So, I said, 'I think I've had enough. I'm not going to throw myself onto the sofa because I've drunk too much. But my submissive friend, if he agrees, is going to put himself on his knees and suck all of you. One by one. Anyone who's not happy, back off.'

Then I looked at him, expecting an answer. He nodded. No one walked away and he got on his knees and obeyed me.

My friend came back over and looked at me, perplexed. 'What is hell is going on here? You're crazy! Are you OK? he asked, laughing.

'I'm just having fun. But I've had too much to drink. Finish fucking whoever you want and we can go.'

'The only one who hasn't fucked here is you, so yes, we can go.'

We laughed and I got up, but I couldn't walk. He escorted me to the changing room, where I passed out.

I woke up the next morning with my hand on my forehead, already feeling a severe headache. He was just finishing packing his bag and looked at me, laughing, saying, 'What a night. I think you need paracetamol.' He gave me some tablets with a glass of water.

I realised I was naked then. 'How did I get here? Why am I naked? Did we have sex last night?'

He laughed. 'No. We did not. Fucking a dead woman is not my thing. After you passed out, I had to carry you in my arms to the taxi, and when we arrived, the doorman helped me get you to the room. Your clothes you took off by yourself.'

'No,' I whispered, putting my head on my pillow.

He left the hotel, as he had a flight to back to America, and I stayed in the room for few more days. I went on some tours and visited the Holocaust Museum, as I am very interested in history.

Tony was constantly texting me, trying to be my friend, saying how much he cared about me, acting very apologetic and always worrying about me being safe.

I missed him; missed his phone calls, his jokes. Apart from his jealousy, everything about him filled me of joy, and I felt loved and not alone. I felt like we were made for each other and I hated my job because I didn't feel I deserved a man.

The life of an escort doesn't have room for a love story, and I was wanting both.

After many texts, we settled on going for dinner and I just felt my legs going when I stood in front of him. My heart started to accelerate and I felt butterflies in my belly. I only had one answer for all this. I loved him.

We had a long conversation during dinner and I was keen to hear from him first. He kept telling me how he wanted to change, to try not to be jealous …

Then we changed the subject, talking about travelling, and he kept looking in my eyes, and, finally, I was just dying to hold him, so I asked, 'So, where are you gonna take me on honeymoon?'

He looked at me and started to cry.

'Are you serious? Are you giving us another chance?'

I held his hand. 'Oh, yes, I want to be with you. We need to try. But you need to promise me you are gonna change. And I will promise you, only another year and I will quit my job.'

He held me then, telling the waiter, 'She wants to be with me. I love her.' And the waiter gave a funny smile as, obviously, he did not care about it. We went to my flat and opened a bottle of prosecco. We were celebrating and, officially, we were now in a relationship.

I woke up and he had already left work. There was a glass of water on my table and a little note: *I love you. Never forget it.* He was my man.

I was so happy. The idea of having him in my life started to change all my plans and I was not feeling alone anymore. But he kept wanting to know everything I was doing and it was hard for me, as I'd been single for twelve years. It was difficult to give someone an explanation about everything I did. He was always worried and wanted to make sure I was safe. I couldn't blame him. If I was on his side, I would never have accepted this situation. He was trying and I needed to seriously consider things.

Mr Handsome invited me for a weekend. Tony didn't like the idea, but I couldn't say no. Not to him. Mr Handsome meant a lot to me. He had been my friend for over four years and it was annoying that Tony was trying to convince me to not go. He told me, 'He is not your friend. He just uses you. Same as all your clients.'

I said, 'Look, I am not going to argue with you. You still go to your house and I trust you when you say you are only going to see your kids. I am so sorry, but I am going. Every weekend, if you are not working, you are with you kids, never with me, and I understand. Do the same for me. It is my job, whether you like or not. It is what I do for living and I asked you for one year.'

That weekend, I didn't have much fun and my behaviour was cold. Obviously, Mr Handsome understood. He always could read my thoughts. Our meetings started to be less and less frequent, until he got another girlfriend, which was the perfect situation for Tony to say, 'See? I told you. You are just a toy. All men just use you.'

After five years with Mr Handsome, it was over. I was feeling a bit disappointed. I missed the hotels, the fun and the company. But it was also fear of change. If I was going to live with Tony though, it was the right thing to do.

36

I gave Tony a key to my flat and we went on a celebratory trip to Turkey. I was bursting with happiness, so excited, and decided to quit my work and not wait another year. It was a surprise and I would only tell him when we were on the trip. I chose a beautiful panorama on the top of a hill, overlooking the sea. 'Once we land in London, I am quitting my job and you can move in with me.'

'You said another year, you still need some money.'

'I will be OK. I've made the decision. I don't want to argue anymore about my work.'

We came back home and he went see his kids and told me he was going sleep over with them. He arrived home the day after. I was in the kitchen cooking and I gave him a kiss. He was very pale and nervous.

I asked him, 'What is happening? Are you OK?'

'My wife found out about us. She saw the flight reservation in your name and she knows your email.'

'What? What do you mean? Doesn't she know we are living together?'

He put his head down without answering my question.

I got nervous. I had a knife in my hand, so I approached him and said: 'I asked you a question; does she know that we are together? Look at me!'

He looked at me and said, 'No, she doesn't.'

'Are you still with your wife? What do you tell her when you are here?' I kept asking him.

'She thinks I'm at work. She probably already knew, or suspected, but she has been waiting for the right moment.'

'Are you kidding me? So, what about your night shift? Do you really work at night?' I asked, and he put his head down again. I started to scream, 'Answer my question and look at me!'

I felt desperation when he replied. 'No. I never do night shifts. When I leave here, I go back home to my family.'

I tightened my grip on the knife in my hand, feeling out of my mind and starting to scream hysterically and point the knife at him. 'Get out of my home! Get away from me! Have you any idea what I have done and given up for you? Get out!'

He just disappeared. I was hysterical.

I couldn't even cry. My first thought was that it was not possible. My man, the person who was so patient with me, who never lost control, who understood me. He was my soulmate, my peace. With so many men available, I chose him.

'No, it must be a nightmare, a misunderstanding. Tomorrow, everything will be clear. He will come back.'

'He is coming back now! He is coming!' I kept telling myself.

But he was not. I left my cooking and burst into tears on the floor. Later, I had to take a tablet to sleep.

In the morning, I opened my eyes, hoping the whole thing was just a nightmare, but he still hadn't come home and, instead, of a 'Good morning' message on my phone, I received an email:

Did you know he was married when you slept with my husband?

I was glad she didn't know about what I did for living.

My world fell down. I have sex every f...ng day with married men. But never without getting money. I never brought a married man into my personal life. It was my rule and I never made that mistake or made an exception. Now I found I was living with a person who had a double life.

I replied to her:

I knew he was married and had children. But I really thought you and he were not together anymore. I don't know what to say. I am confused at the moment. Do you both still have any intimacy?

Yes, we do. We are a happy family and you just destroyed that.

I am very sorry. I didn't know. I won't see him anymore. I promise.

Are you kidding me? You are my husband's mistress. So now you can have him.

To be honest, I was happy to hear that. I did not want to lose him.

He texted me:

I know I made a big mistake. I was too scared of losing you and my kids are very important. But I truly love you and now, she has put me out of the house. I am free if you want me. I am not asking you for forgiveness. I am just asking you to accept me again.

And I did. I told him, 'Come home. We will talk; we always resolve things. My life is not perfect either. I also lie to people who I love.'

My life is a lie. And I needed to lie well. And now I was facing a lie against me, much worse than mine. But I accepted it. I didn't care about judgments; I wanted to give it a try. He was important to me. We spent another couple of weeks together, but then he didn't sleep at home for a few days.

As expected, I got another email from her:

He told me he is not seeing you anymore. So, we decided to give it another chance. My daughter is having a hard time. She needs her father, but I need you to confirm that it is true that you haven't been seeing him anymore and to promise me you won't.

Honestly, the two kids are what made hold my silence. I was about to destroy his marriage, but I was not that person. I don't destroy marriages, especially when kids are involved. I sell sex for mostly married men, but I never went out and had any affair outside the business. I don't cross that line.

No, I never saw him again. I am glad you forgave him and I promise you that he will never see me or hear my voice again. But he has the keys to my house and I want them back. Just post them to me.

Of all men I knew, Tony was the most calculating. He chose me, studied all my weaknesses and what I needed and he built the man of my dreams. Everything he told me was a lie. His job, his life, even his nationality. Every day, he lied about what he was doing. My heart was smashed and I was feeling so stupid.

I lied to all the world, but not to him. He knew everything about me. It made me so angry. I blocked him on my phone and across all my social media. I felt so devastated. I needed a break from everything. I went on long walks by the Thames but, after a few days, I had to go back to my work. 'Let's take some bookings.'

Susy came to see me. I need to get it out; she was my best friend and a person who would never judge me or say things like, 'How could you be so stupid?' or 'How did you never suspect? I told you so!' She would never tell me what I was feeling. I had been questioning her choices, thinking she was wrong, and that I was in a better situation.

No, she just listened and gave me her shoulder to cry on. OK, and she did give me a cynical smile.

We were talking and I was cooking for us. I didn't have any wine, so we decided to go out to buy some drinks. I grabbed my key and the door slammed shut behind me. When we came back, I couldn't put my key in the lock and I realised there were some traces of glue around it and on the floor. I called security and they had to drill the lock to open my door, as there was silicone inside it.

'Someone came with probably a syringe with silicone and inserted it inside the hole,' the maintenance man said.

Then the manager of the building arrived to talk to me.

'We are calling the police.'

'Can I see the cameras?'

'No. you can't. I can't show you the cameras.'

'So how can I know who did it, if I can't see a camera to see if I recognise them?'

'The police will do the work.'

'If I can't see the cameras, I don't want the police here.'

'It is not your choice. I have already called the police.'

'It is my choice to not talk to the police. I won't talk.'

The police arrived, did the paperwork and asked me if I had any suspects.

'No idea who it could be. Can I see the cameras? Maybe I might recognise someone,' I asked them.

'I am afraid not. It is against privacy laws.'

'So, I am afraid it is just paperwork with no result, then. It just fills up your files.'

I was feeling panic, my anxiety was high and I needed tablets to sleep. I went to stay with my daughter and she made me write a letter. A self-statement directing the police, which she keeps in a safe place. She helped me with it. We wrote that if anything happens to me, the police have to investigate Tony as the first suspect. I included his full name, place of work and address on it. I didn't think there was more I could do about it.

37

I sent an email to Tony's wife:

Someone put glue in the hole of my door and I found out yesterday when I couldn't open it. Would you tell me where Tony has been in the last couple of days?

She replied: *Two days ago, we went to the beach. And, yesterday, he was at home with the kids.*

I am really sorry. I only needed to be sure it wasn't him, as the police are around. In this case, he has nothing to do with it. I won't disturb you anymore.

The next morning, I got another email. This time it was from Tony and he was very angry:

What did you text my wife, she will not tell me. She is accusing me of putting glue on your door. I didn't glue your fucking door. And now it's my turn. Your whole family, your mum and dad are going to know what you do. I love you and you are with somebody else that is gluing your door. But now I will show you. Your lies will end now too. I'm not lying to you about anything. Some other fuck buddy is playing games with you, not me.

I did not reply to him.

My morning breakfast was now served with constant emails, one after the other:

She is leaving me. She decided to go for real because of what happened and because of you. So, in the end, I lost everything. And I have nothing to lose, now you do. And if you want to tell her I paid for you as a prostitute, go ahead it's not going to change anything, I'm not scared anymore. You are. The truth on both sides needs to come out. You also put me in a situation where I was leaving and then pulled out, causing family problems for me. And you walk away happy. Sorry, it doesn't work that way. Now it's my turn to do what you did to me. I will destroy your life.

I didn't recognise the person who was writing all these awful things. It was not him. Not Tony. I would never have talked about him to the police because Tony would never do that to me. This must be another person; that is what I thought, and I feared that person.

I had to reply, with lies of my own:

About the camera, it will take a bit of time, they need a court letter to check, but, about your wife, I never told her that was you. I just said that I found glue in my door lock and I need to find who it was. I had to call the management because the door needed to be forced to open and if she could tell me where you were on Wednesday afternoon until Thursday around 5ish. She said you all were at the beach on Wednesday and Thursday you spent all day at home with the kids. I already apologised to her. I don't see why she fears for you if you were home. Unless she was covering for you. Now, you only need to prove to her where you were, not to me anymore. Very simple.

Don't tell me I destroyed your life and what you built, because with me, you only built lies. You had all this time a double life and lied to both of us, and when I found out, I told you and gave you another chance to stop. I said it was the last chance. And you kept doing it. So, it is you who caused all this trouble and now is paying for that. Stop blaming me.

Just because I spoke to your wife doesn't mean I have done anything wrong. We just clarified your lies. You weren't stopping having a double life with both of us. We all three are involved in your lies.

But to tell me you are going to use my family and send links to whoever to destroy me is wicked and it is harassment. If you do that, then yes, you will destroy my life. But I promise you, I will take you with me. She wants me to tell her the truth. So, here is the deal: you send a picture of my profile to my family and she will receive one. Send 100 of my pictures, she will receive 100. This includes a screenshot of my pictures and videos of us fucking and all letters of love during of this time. I still have the message from four years ago when you booked me for the first time. She doesn't need to know the truth, because she won't be happy to know that her husband fell in love with a prostitute, or how you called me, with a such dirty profile, who invites men to come to fuck my arse as I have. So please, after reading this email, do not reply to me. Don't contact me anymore. We are just creating more pain for all of us. Do you really think it is worth it to keep doing this?'

It was so painful to talk to him like that. I couldn't do it anymore. I needed a break to pick up the pieces of myself and put them together again, to get the power to turn the page. He was not the person who I fell in love with. He was not the person who I wanted to be with. I gave up my life as a 'prostitute' as he called me, for him. I deserved better.

If I decide to stop my work for someone, I want it to be someone I can take care of, and vice versa. Someone who is mine. What is the point of being a mistress and having the job I have? I'm already getting a good amount of money serving married men. It would be foolish to have this responsibility on my back in my personal life, too.

In one of Tony's emails, he asked me why I couldn't accept him being married when most of my clients were. I didn't reply, but, for me, the answer was clear. He wasn't my client.

Covid arrived. The government announced a lockdown and I was so frustrated and afraid of staying at my flat alone. I just closed the door and went to live with my daughter. Living alone at that point was not a good choice.

I thought this might to be a sign that it was time to leave my flat for good. It had been four years, so I needed to change my address. I wrote a notice letter to my landlady and left my flat.

My daughter received me with a big warm hug and I was so desperate to lie on her lap and get some cuddles, as she was so supportive about everything.

I am so proud of my daughter. I look at her and I see a mirror of myself when I was younger; she is just like me, but with a much stronger personality. When I was her age, I left my home and wanted to embrace the world. That was a different time and I didn't have my parents to support me. They couldn't afford to help. Now she has so many dreams and she can achieve anything. She is better than me.

We were having some wine and talking about embracing all of life, when I told her,

'It is about embracing the whole package; the bigger the package, the bigger the result. We learn, we teach, we win, we lose; we are going to be happy, but we are also going to suffer. It is all included in the package. Otherwise, it is easy to stay inside the bubble and live a normal life. It's all about choices.'

We spent three months together. Without her support, I wouldn't have made it. I was taking long walks every day on my own to process things in my head. I was still really missing my kind Tony, but I was also so afraid of the person who was threatening to destroy my life.

As I always believed, forgiveness heals the pain, and I was trying not to be angry. After six months, there is still not a day I don't miss Tony. But there was not a day either that I could forgive the person who had lied to me. The person who I would have trusted my life with, who was constantly in my dreams, now filled me with fear. I regretted not telling the police. I fitted cameras at my daughter's house.

38

During the lockdown, I had spoken to Susy. After three months, we finally were able to hug at the park. She had been doing well with her boyfriend just before the lockdown. She stopped doing escort work for a few months and started working in a friend's coffee shop, just to have something to do in the mornings, as her partner had enough money to support her. I think it was prudent, as she was followed by a private investigator, hired by her boyfriend's ex-wife. She was probably trying to find things to win more in the divorce process. But when the lockdown came, he decided to go to his family's house, afraid of not seeing his children, so she did the same. He never came back.

Susy's husband supported her and stood by her, but if before they were in the last stage of their marriage, now it was over for good.

The government announced the second lockdown in November. 'I don't want to stay here,' I said to my daughter.

'Mum, go to see granny. They are so alone there. I will be fine here.'

I got a flight the day before the second lockdown started on the third of November. I wanted to see my parents. I had spent all my life having issues with my dad, and now I wanted to change things. During this lockdown, I had had time to talk to myself. I wanted to see him, I wanted to tell him, 'I love you,' and I wanted to offer him a trip to see the woman who was the love of his life.

Finally, I was home and happy to see my family. The signs of my dad's age had marked his face, though. A week after my arrival, I was still waiting for the courage and a proper moment alone to have a conversation with my dad. That night, I was in my room talking with Susy on the phone when my mum screamed.

I ran out of my room and saw my dad on the floor. I called the ambulance. He had had a stroke. And that night, it happened three times.

He lived, but he didn't know exactly what was going on, and he needed a wheelchair. Devastated, I made the decision to not come back to London. My heart was so destroyed and I ended up taking care of him, washing and feeding him. It was the only thing left that I could do for him.

'I forget, where is my daughter?' he asked me.

'She is in London, Dad. It is very far,' I replied.

'Are you going back? Do not leave me here.'

'No, I won't. I will stay here. I promise you,' I told him.

'I love you,' I heard him say, for the first time, but I did not say it back. The words got stuck in my throat, almost suffocating me. I couldn't get them out.

My dad passed five weeks later. I stayed with him until his last day, but he never heard 'I love you' from my mouth. It was so devastating and makes me angry at myself.

The loss of my dad changed me completely. It was his time to go, but it wasn't my time to lose him. I waited too long and it was too late.

After coming back to London, I sank into complete sadness for many months. I was having panic attacks. Susy had been working with me, so we were supporting each other, as we both needed to restart our lives and did not like working alone in a flat. We did not care about the law. We were together all the time, even when I had a booking, as my body trembled in panic and Susy put some drops of a natural tranquiliser under my tongue. She had been my best friend during all this. She was living in a small flat and sharing the custody of her kids with her husband. They were doing well and are still very good friends. We were each other's support. This lasted for four or five months until my psychological state stabilised.

And now, I have changed again. I see life in a milder way. I don't rush, but I don't want to waste my time anymore and I am trying to become a better human being.

Almost a year after my dad was put to rest, my mum developed slight dementia. She is fine and she lives in a nice house, paid for by me. I spoil her so much. I bought my mum's forgiveness and she is happy. She takes swimming classes three times a week and feels so healthy. She thinks she is a teenager and when she sees a man, she feels butterflies in her belly. I think it is great, but my sister is not happy about this. She thinks it is too early and she should give it more time before trying to get another man, but I don't think so. Time is a luxury that you don't have when you are seventy-three years old. How many elders get dementia and become miserable? My mum just thinks she is young.

I realised that, doing my job, I don't need a boyfriend. I am happy on my own and my daughter knows everything about what I do.

Now, she has her own business and I couldn't want anything better from her.

She never judges me, but I don't think she is proud of what I do. She doesn't interfere with my life, but she sees me getting older, and she thinks it is time to stop. She wants me to work with her. She says that I did what I had to do to help her make a good life, and now, she wants to return the favour.

What else could a mum expect from a child? She fills me with joy, even if I don't tell her. But now is the time to let her know. I won't wait to tell her every day how much I love her.

She doesn't ask me to stop my work, but she is giving me another choice. We don't live together now. I found another place to live, so, while I am single and seeing clients who I like, it is all good. But I know she wants me to quit.

In my private life, in love, I have spent my entire life, up and down, looking for my Alpha. In my sexual work life, I try to be a strong woman, providing my services, which are mostly about being dominant and in control. I had hidden behind Lily, a character who I built, inspired by the person I wanted to be: strong, naughty, adventurous, in charge and searching for something better. I have learned so much with Lily and I transformed myself into a stronger person, with better self-esteem and financial independence. Exactly as I planned.

In the past, I pressured myself, convincing myself that I needed to find someone to change my life, and that they needed to be the reason to stop my work, for a 'normal life'.

I was so wrong. As a sex worker, my lifestyle is not compatible with a relationship, and I don't need a man in my home because I am happy being single. Only now have I realised that Mr Handsome was right. If I want to stop being a sex worker, I can do it anytime, without using a man as a reason. I can stop just because I want to. And do I want to stop? I'm not sure yet.

I will pay society's consequences in terms of discrimination against what I do. I will never be able to erase my past. I will carry Lily inside me for the rest of my life. But also, I will carry all my great adventures, all the positive things that made me grow up, and all the bad and funny moments which only I have lived inside Lily and couldn't have done with a different body. I will never regret it.

We only live once; life is short. Don't waste a chance, especially a second one. No matter how life is, when we feel unhappy, it's only ourselves who pay for it.

Everything is for sale and we all have a price. Whoever thinks they cannot be bought has just never gotten the right offer.

Printed in Great Britain
by Amazon